by
Les Wise

CONTENTS

The Language of Improvisation	2
How to Use This Book	4
Major Ideas	6
Minor Ideas	17
Dominant 7th Ideas	26
IIm7 V7 Imaj7 Ideas	37
IIm7 V7 Ideas (one bar phrase)	90
Turnarounds	96
Idea Substitution Chart	102
About the Author	103

INTRODUCTION

This book is written for the musician who is interested in acquiring a firm foundation for playing jazz. The ideas presented are from the great musicians who have shaped various facets of the jazz idiom. The developing musician should not merely "memorize licks" but learn to embellish these ideas with his own, forming concepts that ultimately mold an individual style. By building up a vocabulary of these melodic ideas, we can begin connecting them together in endless possibilities to form larger phrases and complete solos.

ISBN 978-0-634-03355-1

7777 W. BLUEMOUND RD. P.O. BOX 13819 MILWAUKEE, WI 53213

Copyright © 1982, 2002 by HAL LEONARD CORPORATION
International Copyright Secured   All Rights Reserved

No part of this publication may be reproduced in any form or
by any means without the prior written permission of the publisher.

Visit Hal Leonard Online at
www.halleonard.com

THE LANGUAGE OF IMPROVISATION

Musical improvisation. Let's define what it is **not**. It is not the God-given ability to invent melodies from out of the sky. It does not come from a bolt of lightening, enabling one to be a monster soloist. It is not a divine gift which only a few of us have because we are special. What, then, is improvisation? It is **spontaneous reorganization**. Think for a moment of what those two words mean—"the rearrangement of something that already exists." It is learned in much the same way that a language is because musical improvisation is a language. We all have the ability to learn the language of improvisation; it's simply a matter of proper direction.

Let's examine what a language is. When we speak, we do not instantly invent the words which flow from our mouth. They already exist. Likewise, when we solo we use patterns and ideas which already exist in the language of music.

The average high school graduate is said to know about 15,000 words. Yet two individuals may express completely separate ideas, thoughts, and opinions while using the same set of words. How is this so? Simply by arranging these words in different orders. If we're all operating within the same basic structural vocabulary, then it's the order in which we reorganize the words that give our personality a uniqueness which we call our own.

When we speak, we generally do so intuitively, and it seems to be an automatic process. Yet if we think back and analyze the development of our vocabulary, we see that it really was not. The process of learning to solo is much the same way. Let me point out some of the similarities.

Speech development, up until we entered school, was by imitation. Our parents spoke a word or a phase, and we simply repeated it. In the same manner, before we ever had a music teacher or knew a thing about music, we simply imitated sounds. We may have heard a melody from a television or radio commercial and attempted to imitate that melody on our instrument.

In the first grade we learned a word. We not only learned how to pronounce the word but how the individual letters symbolize the sounds that form the word. We learned how to spell it and how to write it on the blackboard. To further complicate matters, we had to learn the meaning of the word and how to use it in a sentence. The parallel drawn to our instrument is fairly obvious. In our music lessons we began to learn about some chords, scales, and arpeggios. We learned what notes they consist of, what they sound like, and where they are used. Our test as musicians was to play before an audience—our parents or friends. Our test from our school teacher was to read our story containing our newly learned words to the rest of the class.

With the onset of junior High School, further additions increased our understanding of the English language. I'm sure we all must remember sentence diagramming—now wasn't that just loads of fun? All kinds of lines and arrows were pointing in all directions at words and under words and over words. In complete confusion we thought to ourselves, "So this represents the intuitive speech of one human being communicating to another? How can something so contrived and formulated be any part of just plain everyday communication?" Yet as we learned about our language, the formula became more and more clear, and during the educational process we picked up word after word. One at a time they were added—some from English, some from math, some from history, and some from science. Our vocabulary grew tremendously and usually without much effort.

Now imagine the horror if on your first day of school, the teacher began by handing out enormous books and saying, "Here is a book containing the 15,000 words that you must know by the time you leave the twelfth grade." You would have wanted to go home right then and there. Yet fortunately it didn't happen that way, and instead we learned our language one day at a time. Our verbal communication was a natural, growing, intuitive process.

As word after word was added, the process became so subtle that we now can hardly even remember when and where we learned specific words. Take the word "aluminum" for example. When did you learn it? Was it third grade? fifth grade? eighth grade? Chances are you can't remember. As you went through life acquiring new words, you didn't worry about them, grasp onto them, or hang them around your neck and build your entire life around them. They subtly crept into your vocabulary, and you began to use them intuitively and automatically.

Let's imagine a not so automatic use of communication. Suppose you went to Russia and were suddenly approached by a Russian on the street. The five Russian words you had memorized on the flight over would have to suffice in order to communicate at all. Now don't you think that your speech would sound a bit contrived and mechanical? Would it be at all expressive, intuitive, or automatic? Those five Russian words would be overused, abused, misused, and completely exhausted within one minute. Not to mention the great effort you would employ in attempt to speak these words in some coherent order. Yet, if you knew 15,000 Russian words, you would simply relax and communicate. The process of how to arrange these words would no longer feel contrived, but completely automatic, or—improvised.

We build our vocabulary on our instruments much as we built our English vocabulary. We slowly and gradually add new licks. Some we may read, some we learn from records, some we copy from a friend. We use what already exists—we copy and imitate. You may ask, "But how can I be original and have my own distinct style if I imitate others?" Well, let me ask you, "Did you reject your first words from your mother and father because you invented your own language?" Of course not. You didn't argue the fact that the object which lifts food into your mouth is called a spoon. Our distinct personality is expressed by the order in which we arrange the words which are common to us all. In music, we may play something that seems completely new and unique. But in reality it's a combination of ideas we already know. It may be four consecutive notes we learned three years ago, combined with part of a lick we took from a record last week. We play this idea and believe that we've stumbled upon something totally new, and in a sense we have. It's a reorganization of that which already existed.

Let's look at another way in which vocabulary is expanded. Have you ever been sitting with a group of friends when somebody used a word that caught your attention? You didn't know the exact meaning of the word, but you knew you had heard it somewhere before, and now by the nature of the sentence your friend used, you understand instantly what the word means. Within this same instant you may have realized you liked the word, made a mental note of it, then put it completely out of your mind. The next day you were talking to a friend, and "zap"—the same word came out. Once you are proficient at the language of musical improvisation, the same process will happen. You'll step on the bandstand, not knowing what you will play, and the ideas will flow out. You'll remember a lick you heard from a piano player last week and you'll find yourself playing it. You will have learned enough patterns and shapes and combinations of ideas to play this same lick which had been residing in your subconscious mind. Or you may take a few notes of the same lick and combine it with another which you copied from a saxophone player five years earlier. The musical ideas are already in existence, but the way in which you rearrange these ideas will express your own style and personality—just as when you speak. Your unique personality is the order in which you string all the ideas together.

Musical improvisation is a language, just as English, French, Spanish, and German are languages. It has to be learned. Sure it can and will eventually feel natural and "improvised," but it first must be learned in the same contrived manner that we learned our own language or in the same contrived way that we would learn any new language—one word at a time. It sounds free and easy, but is acquired over a lifetime. One new lick or idea at a time—what it is made of, where to use it and what it communicates or expresses. To increase our ability to communicate on our instrument, we increase our musical vocabulary. To increase our musical vocabulary we learn new licks. We play them over and over until they are habits—until our fingers play them independently of our conscious mind—until we can play them in our sleep, with or without our instruments. Repetition. Where do we get them from? Copy records, copy friends, copy friend's records. From transcriptions, from other instruments—one new word or phrase at a time. Then another and another. This is the process by which we learn and expand the language of improvisation.

HOW TO USE THIS BOOK

This book will solve two of the most common problems among musicians. 1) The lack of a strong musical vocabulary (licks, patterns, etc.) and 2) How to connect the ideas into smooth solos once they have been memorized.

You will notice that the book not only contains melodic ideas to be played over individual chord (major, minor, and dominant) but also a great number of larger musical sentences for chord progressions (i.e., IIm7–V7–Imaj7 and turnarounds. i.e., Imaj7–VI7–IIm7–V7).

All the ideas are categorized into sections for easy reference and also the starting note (in interval notation) for every idea is given (root, 3rd, 5th, 7th, etc.). This will enable you to use the ideas more quickly in your playing.

One way to give our solos continuity is to memorize musical sentences. The next step is to connect these sentences into paragraphs. Here's how we do it. In the IIm7–V7–Imaj7 section of the book the melodic ideas are grouped according to the starting note of the IIm7 chord (the root of a Dm7 chord is D, the ♭3rd is F, the 5th is A, etc.). Also notice that the note the IIm7–V7 (Dm7–G7) resolves to when it reaches the Imaj7 (Cmaj7) chord is indicated in interval notation. This is shown because if we wanted to connect the IIm7–V7 line to another progression or add another idea, it's important to know the starting note (interval) of the next idea for it to connect smoothly.

EDITOR'S NOTE: Audio ends at track 82 due to CD time limitations.

MUSICAL EXAMPLES

WORD

SENTENCE

PARAGRAPH

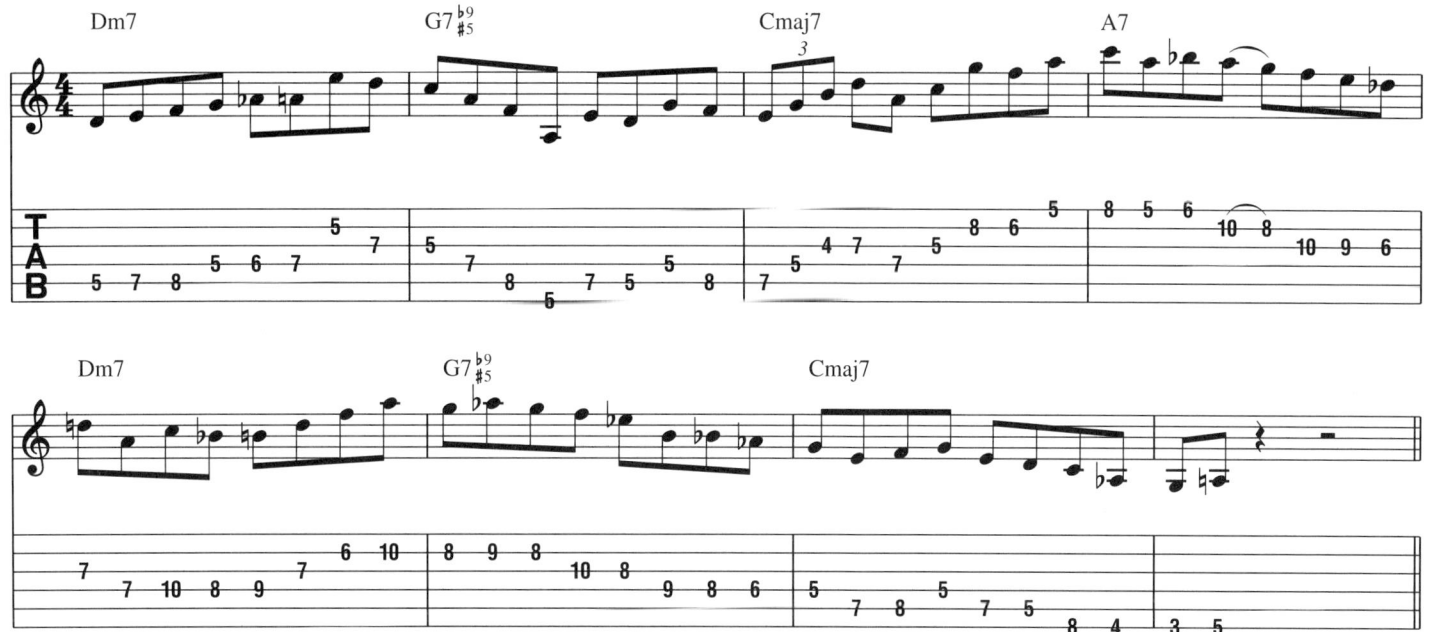

The lines in the "Bebop Bible" are written as straight eighth notes for easy reading, but to play the ideas in a "bop" swing fashion the eighth notes should be phrased like this:

Here are some tips for you to think about as you go through the book.

1. Learn small sections at a time, maybe four or eight notes.
2. Play slowly to ensure correct programming of motor skills.
3. Transpose the ideas to all keys.
4. Learn the ideas in different octaves.
5. Practice singing the lines away from your instrument.
6. Tape the chord changes and play the ideas against them.
7. Experiment with breaking up the lines rhythmically.
8. Incorporate the ideas into your playing immediately.

MAJOR IDEAS
Starting on the Root

1

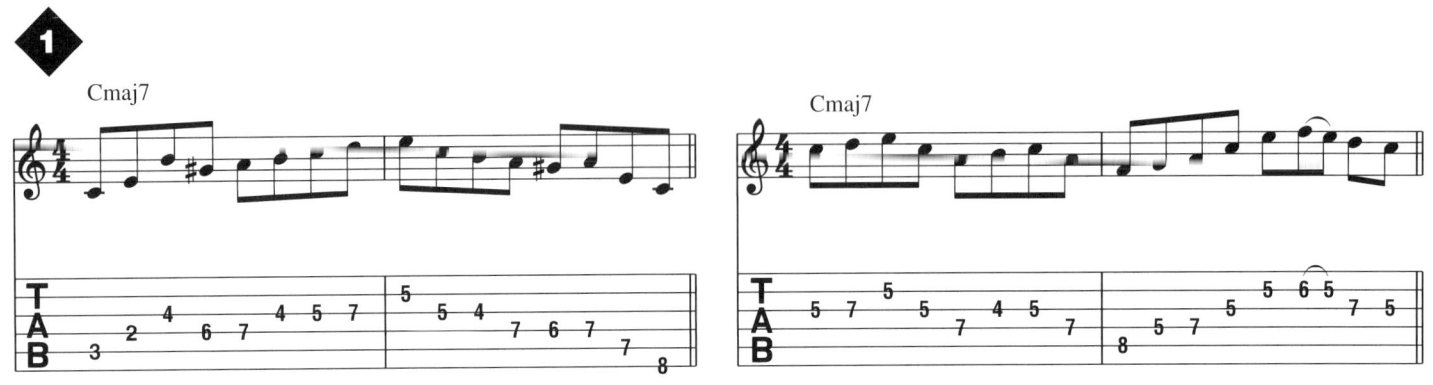

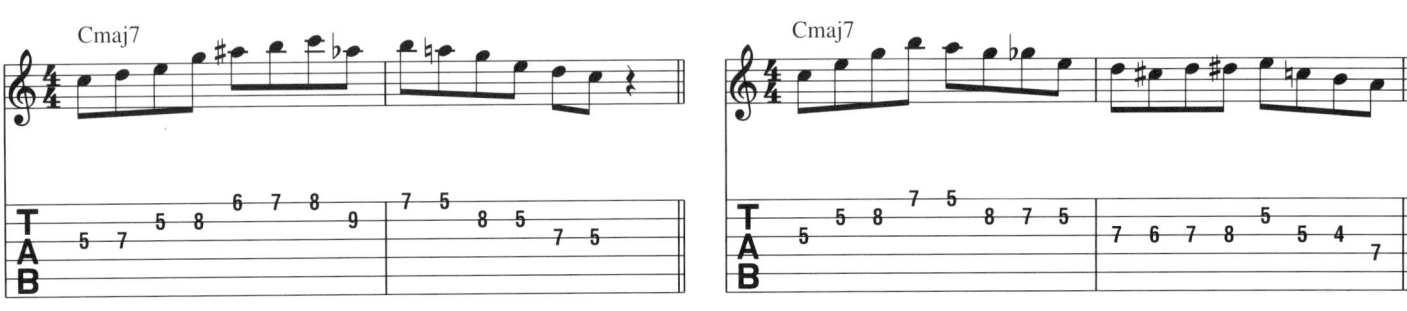

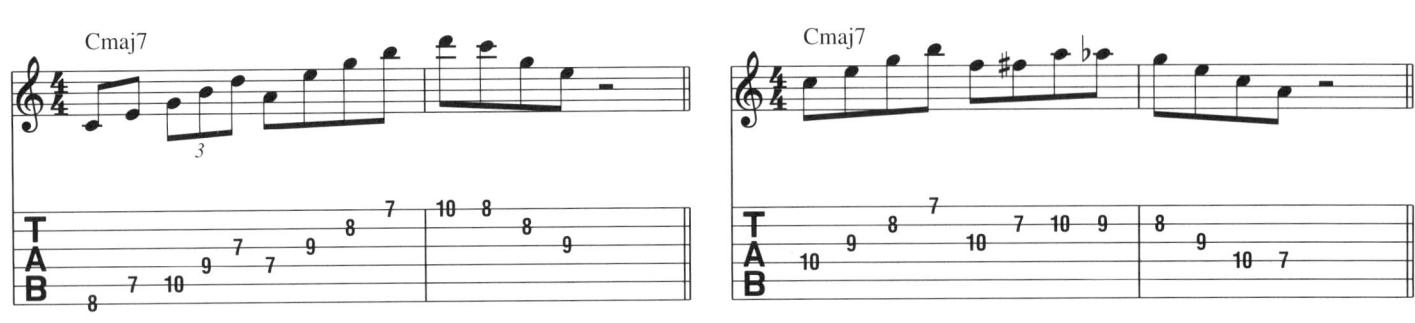

Major Ideas Starting on the Root

Major Ideas Starting on the Root

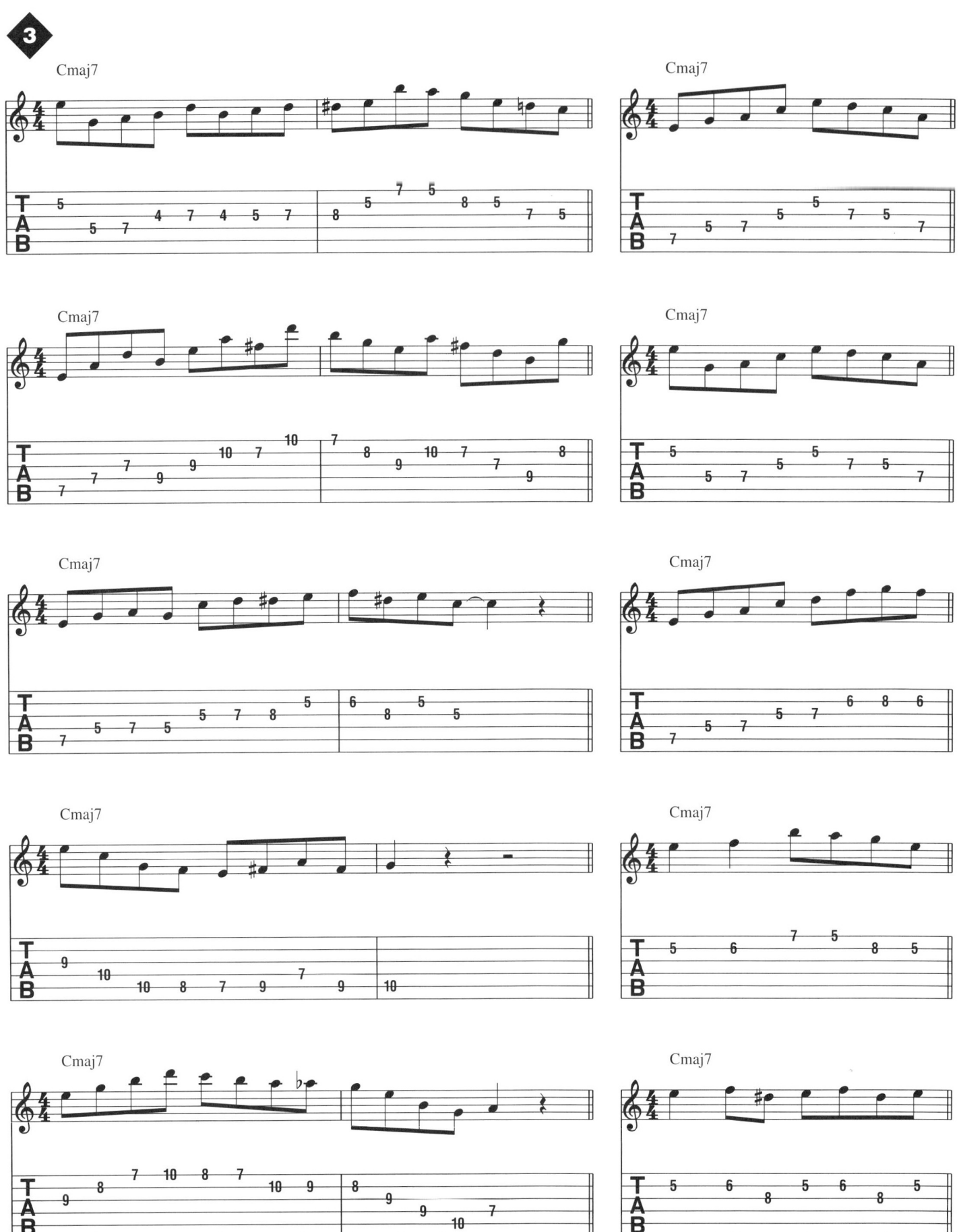

Major Ideas Starting on the Root

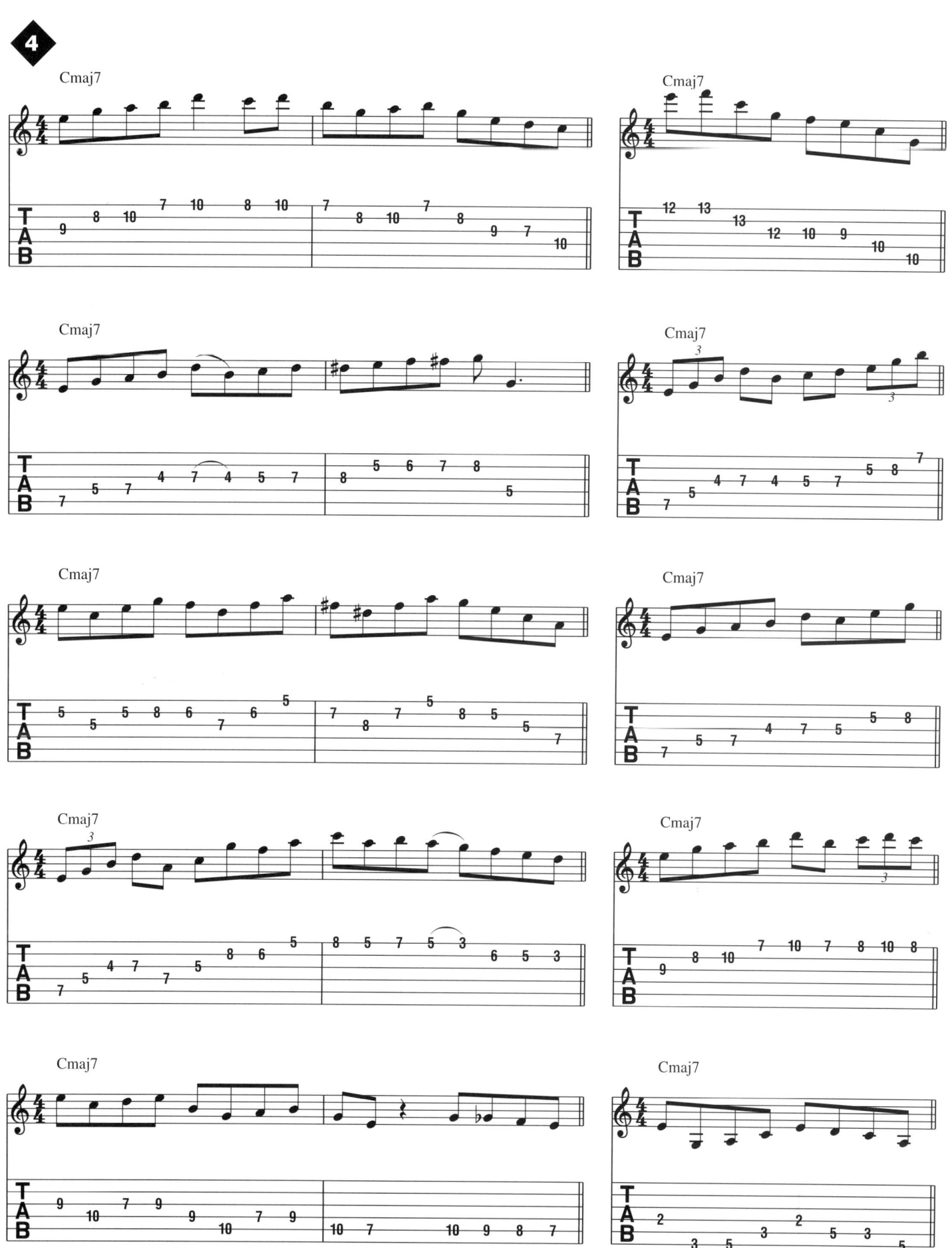

Major Ideas Starting on the Root

MAJOR IDEAS
Starting on the 4th or 11th

MAJOR IDEAS
Starting on the 5th

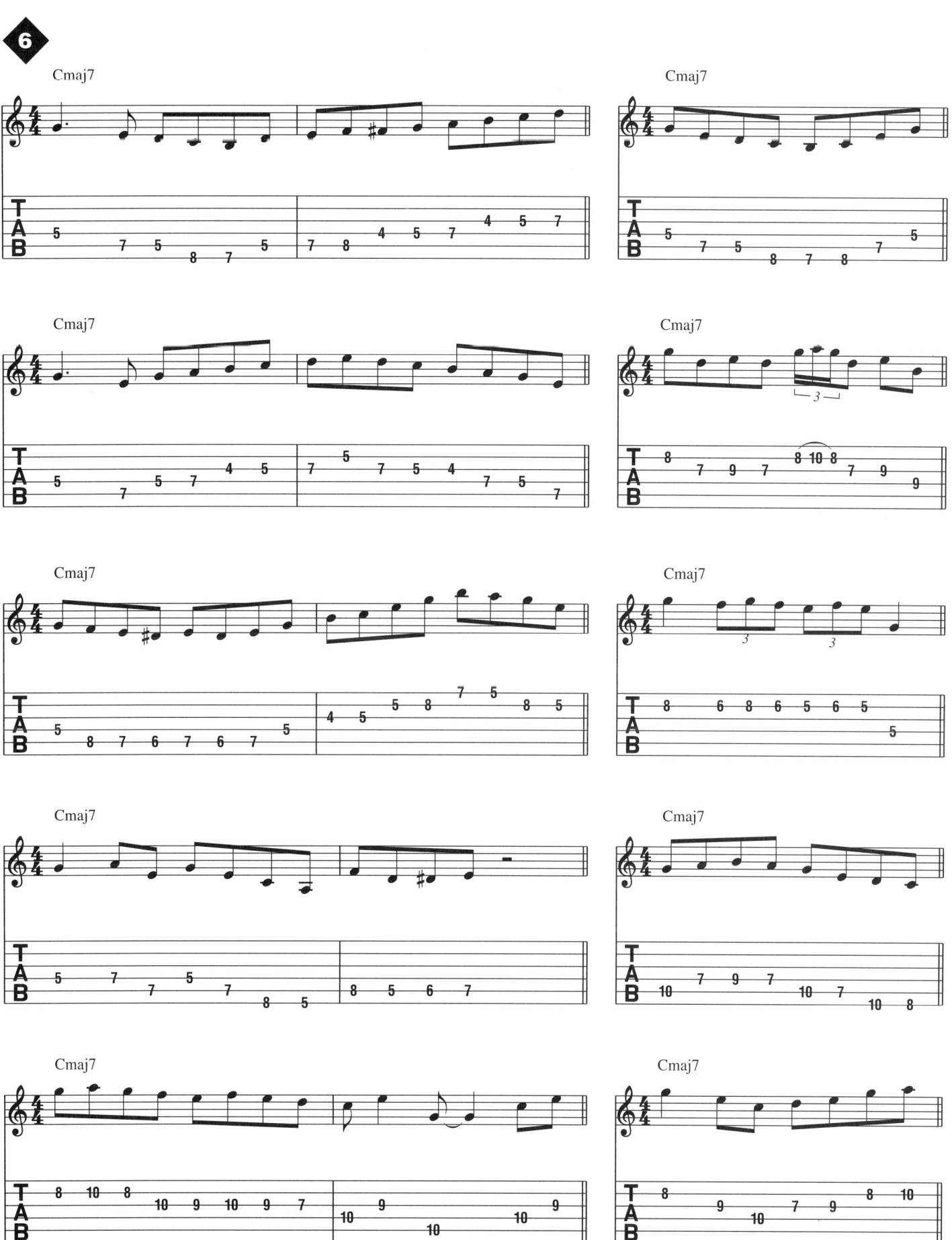

Major Ideas Starting on the 5th

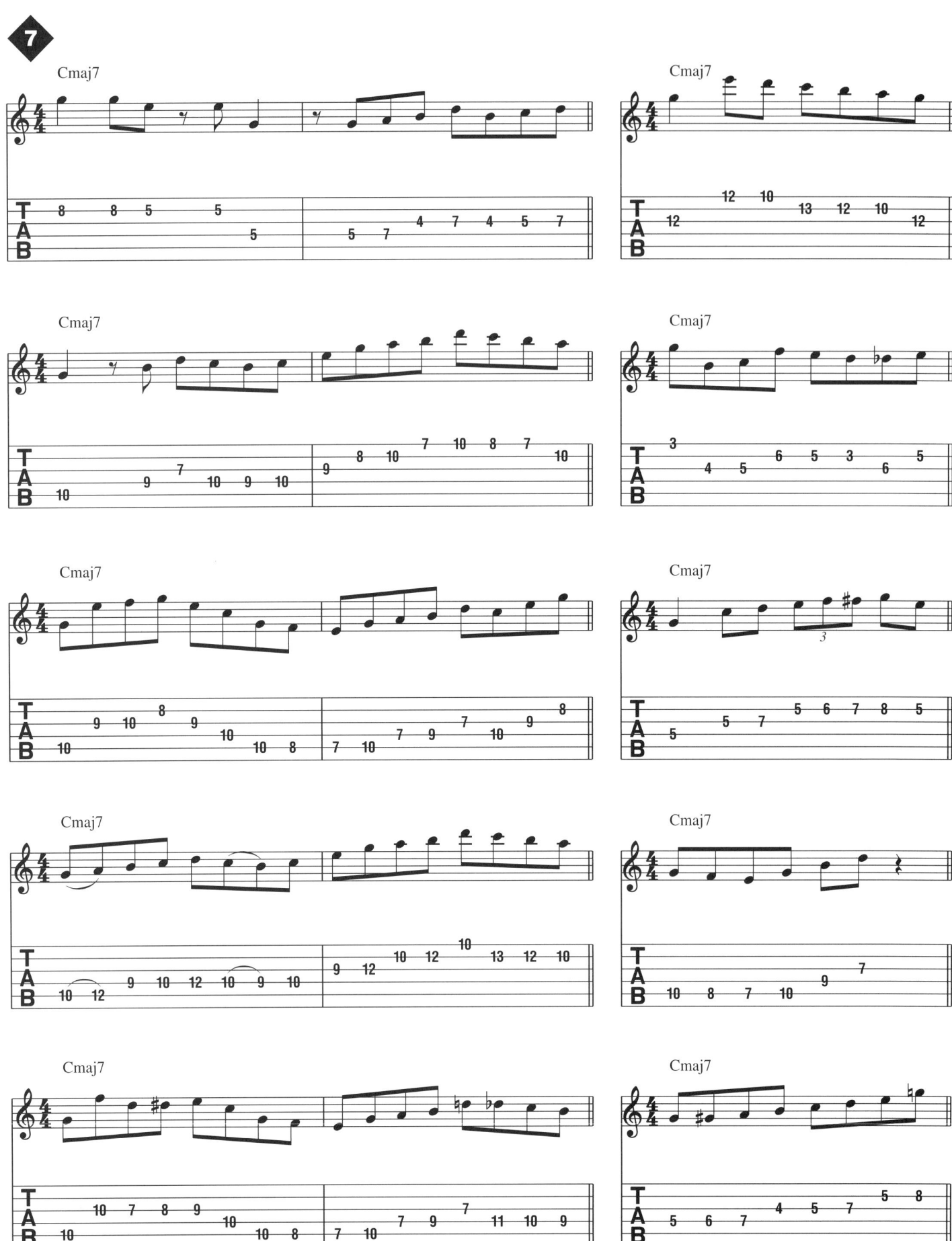

Major Ideas Starting on the 5th

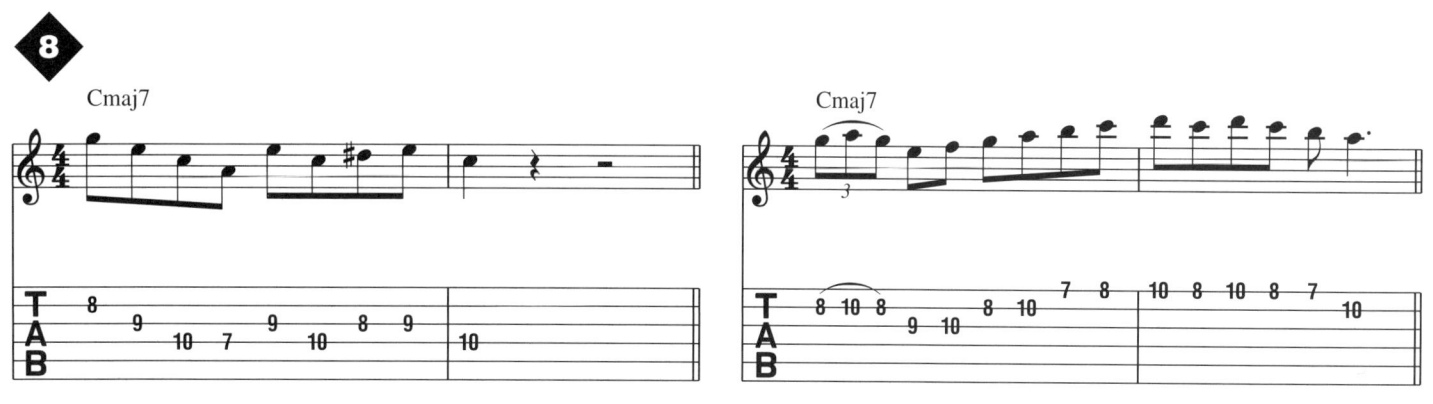

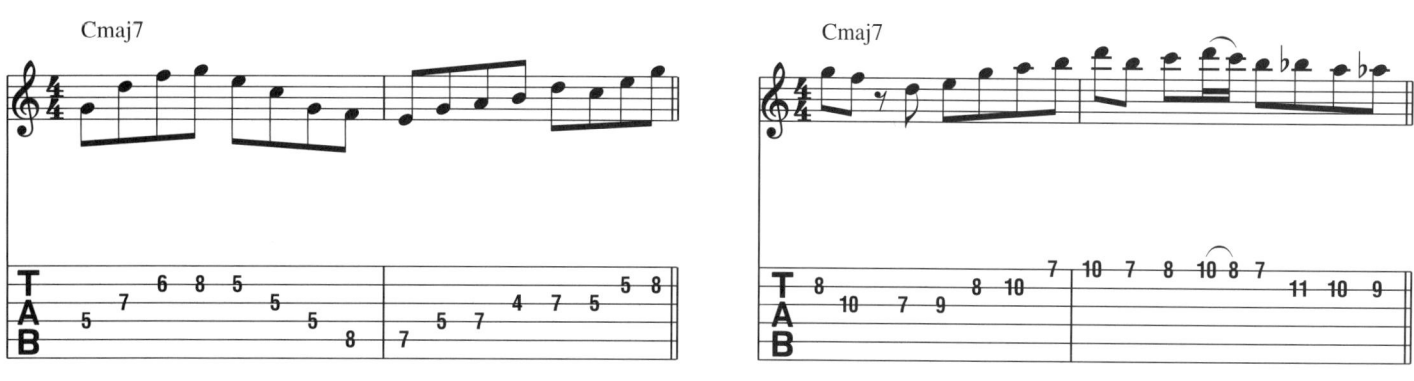

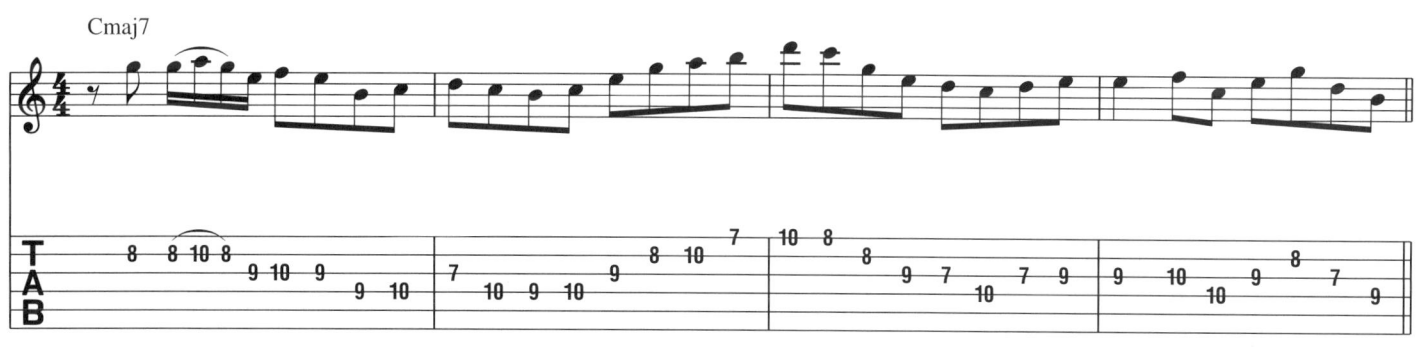

MAJOR IDEAS
Starting on the 6th or 13th

9

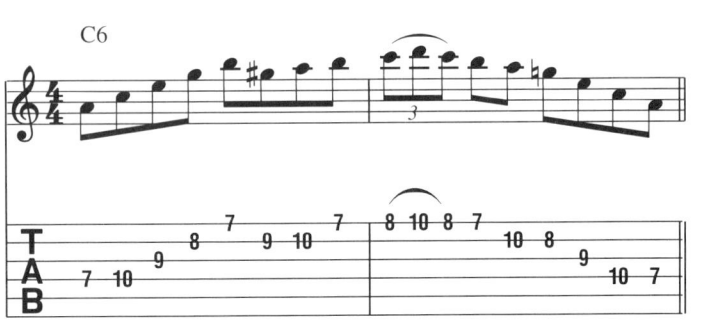

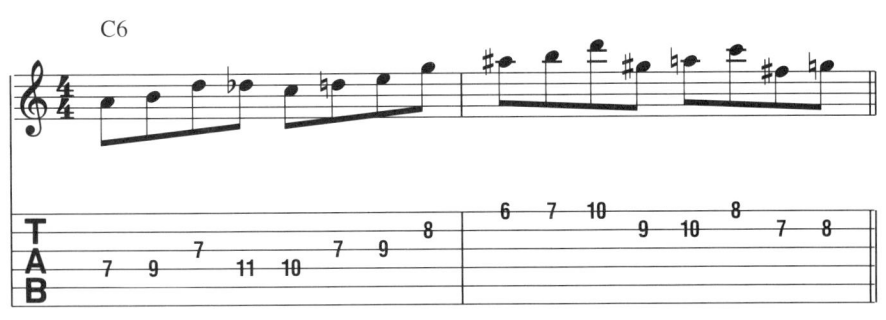
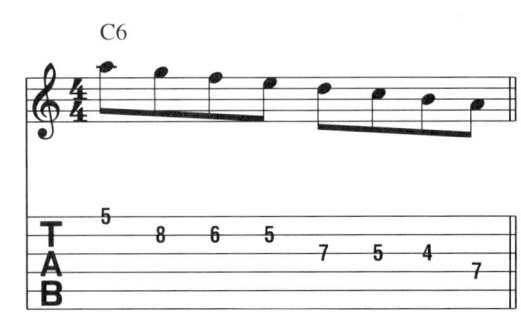
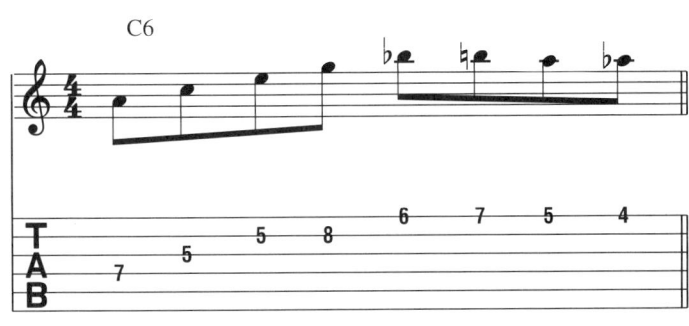

MAJOR IDEAS
Starting on the 7th

MAJOR IDEAS
Starting on the 2nd or 9th

11

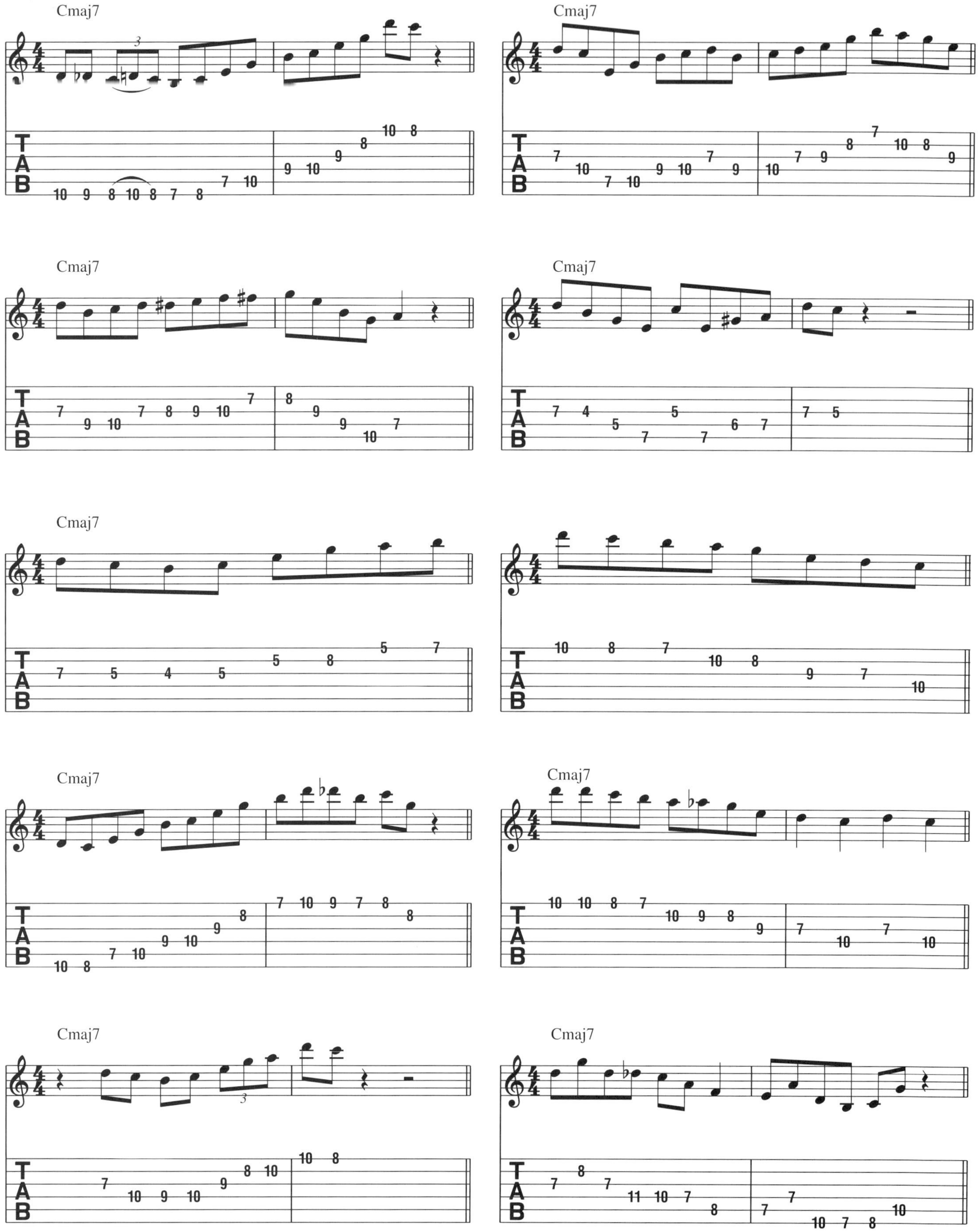

MINOR IDEAS
Starting on the Root

◆ 12

Minor Ideas Starting on the Root

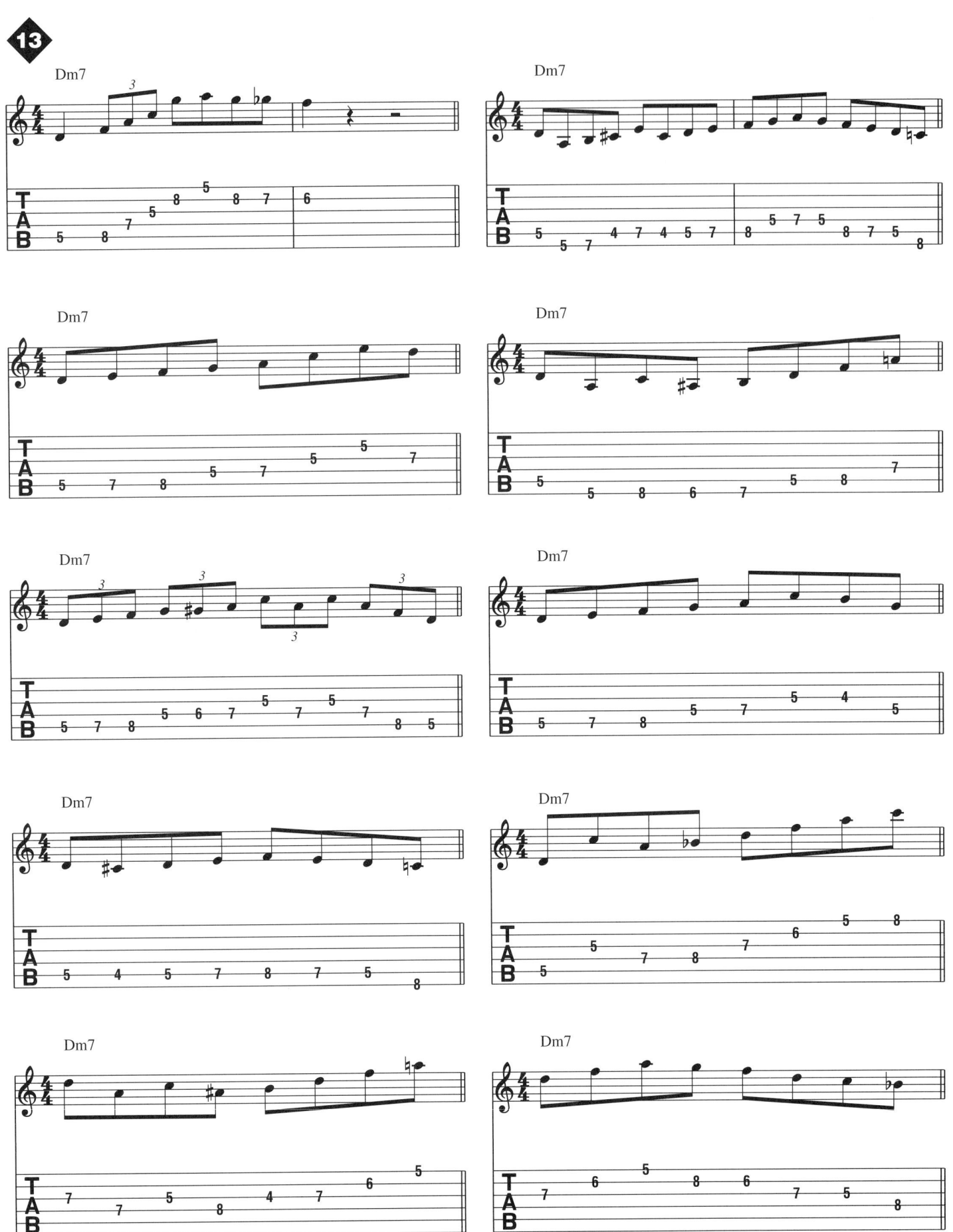

MINOR IDEAS
Starting on the ♭3rd

14

Minor Ideas Starting on the ♭3rd

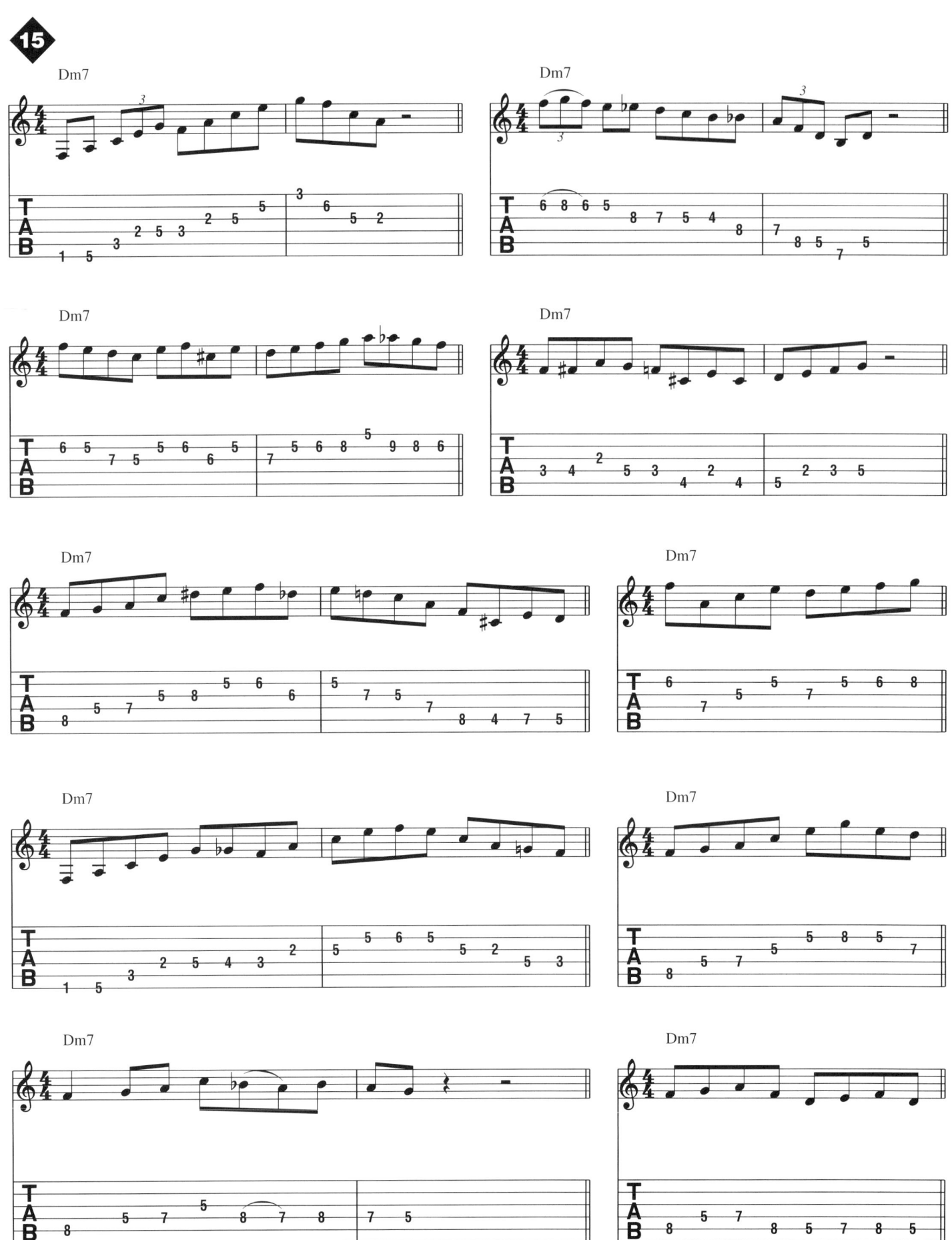

MINOR IDEAS
Starting on the 4th or 11th

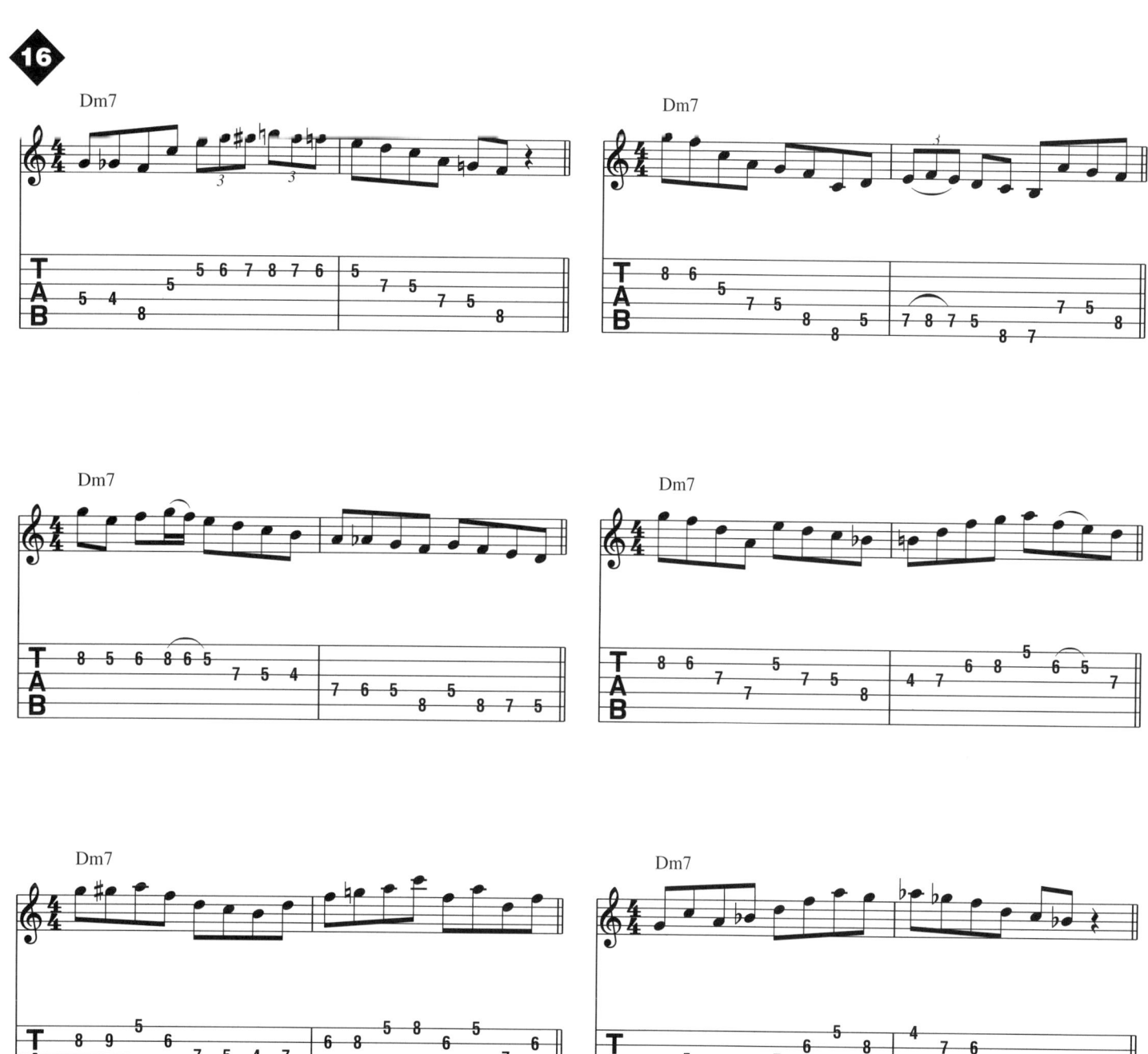

21

MINOR IDEAS
Starting on the 5th

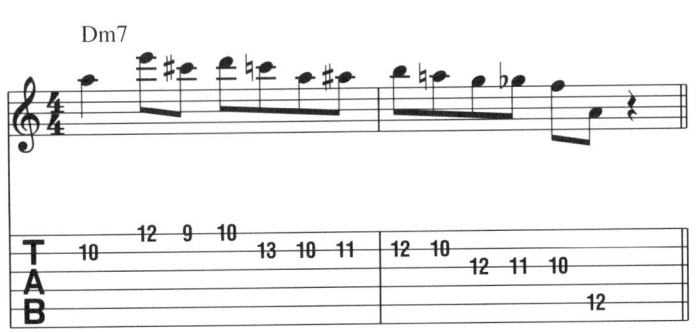

Minor Ideas Starting on the 5th

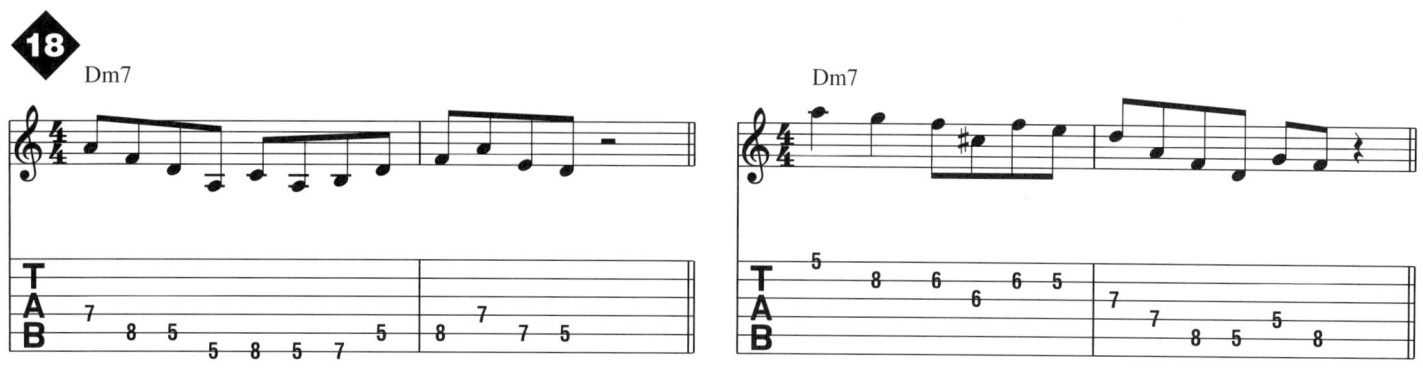

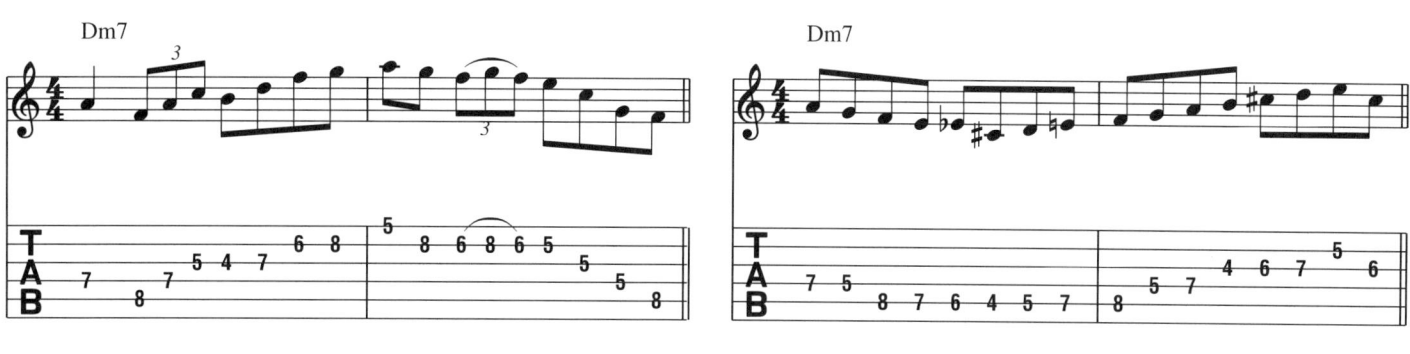

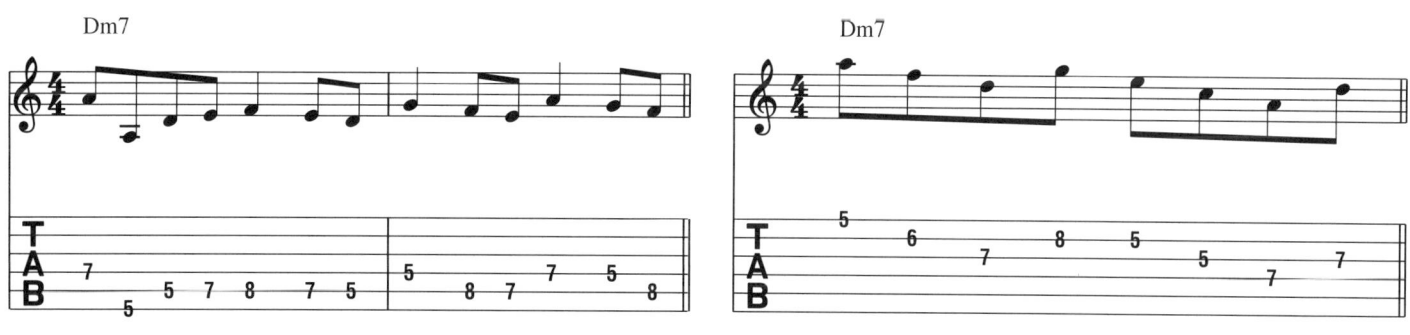

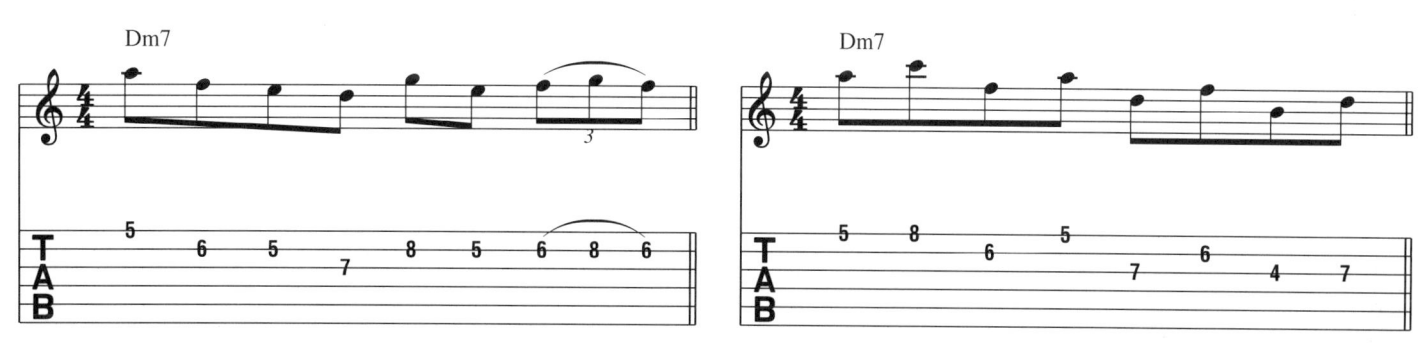

MINOR IDEAS
Starting on the 6th or 13th

19

MINOR IDEAS
Starting on the ♭7th

20

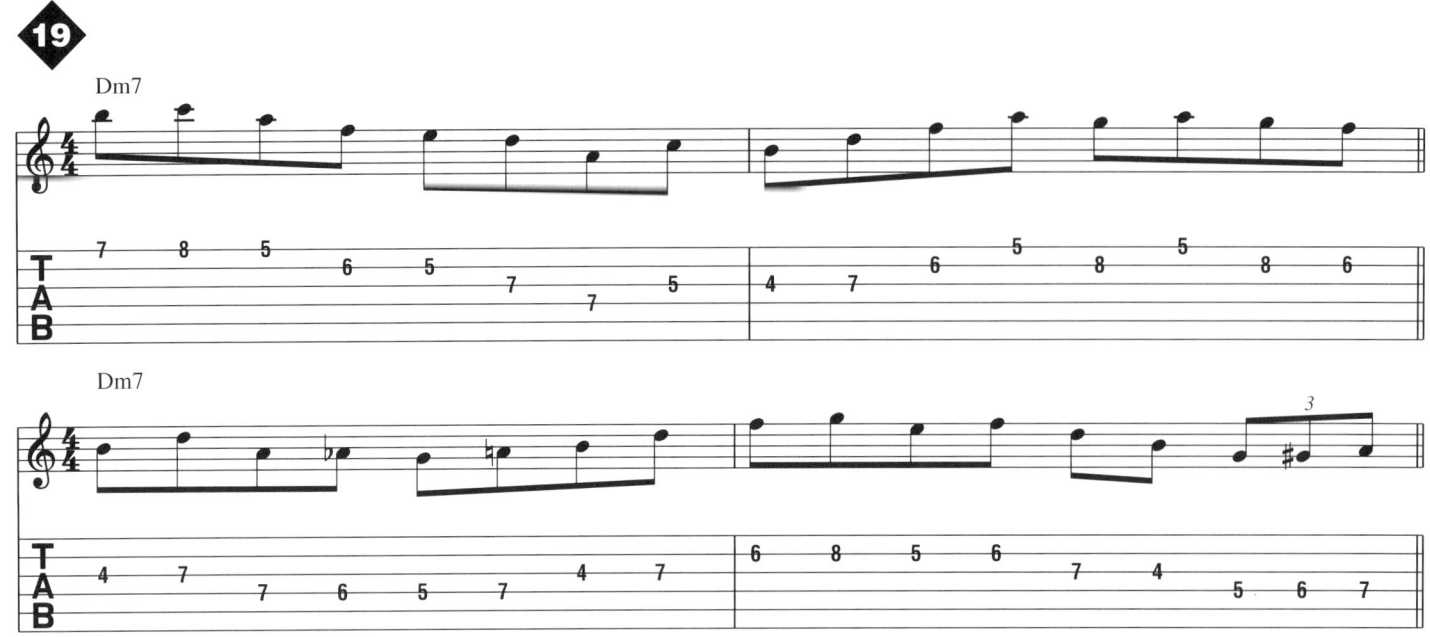

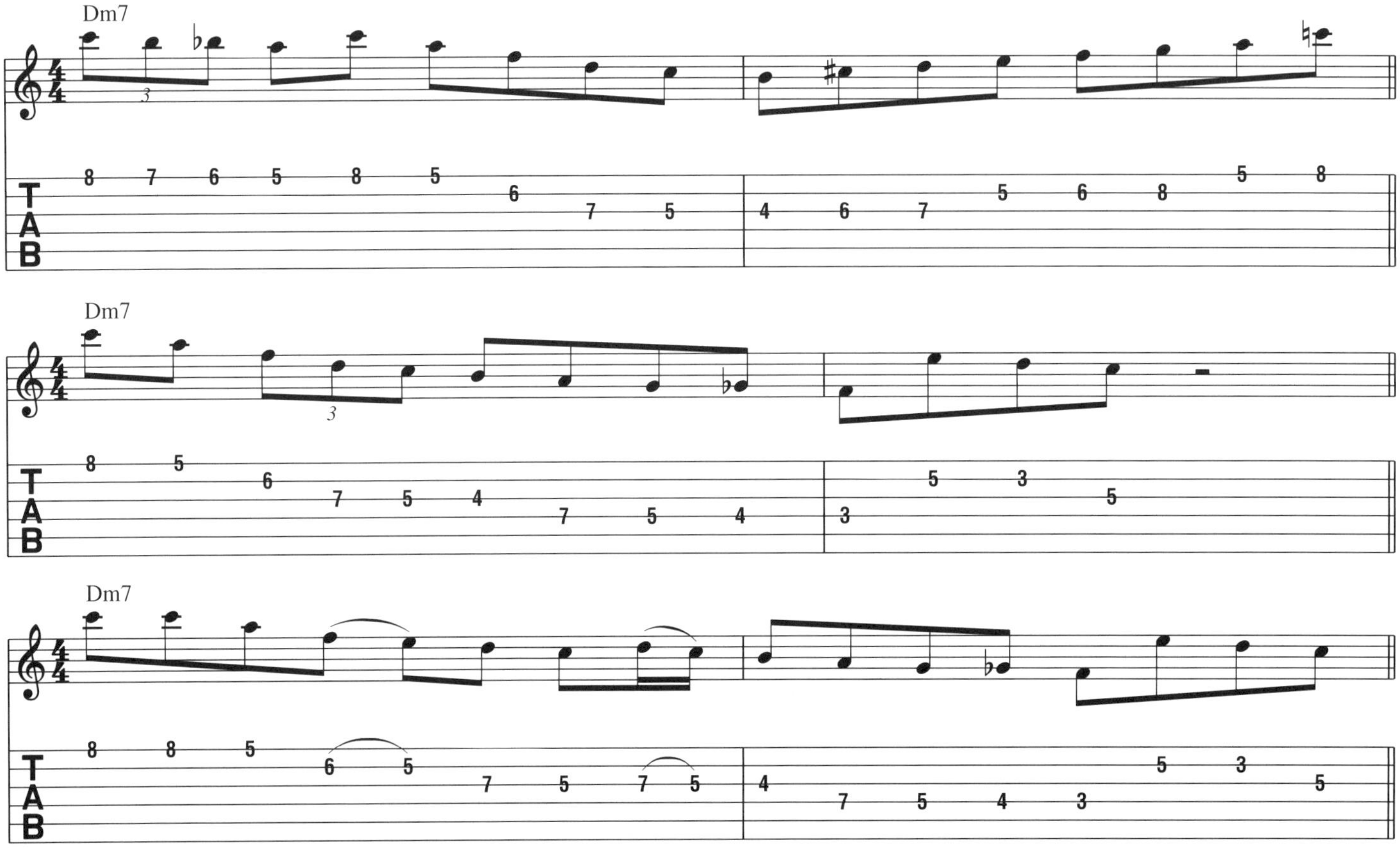

MINOR IDEAS
Starting on the 2nd or 9th

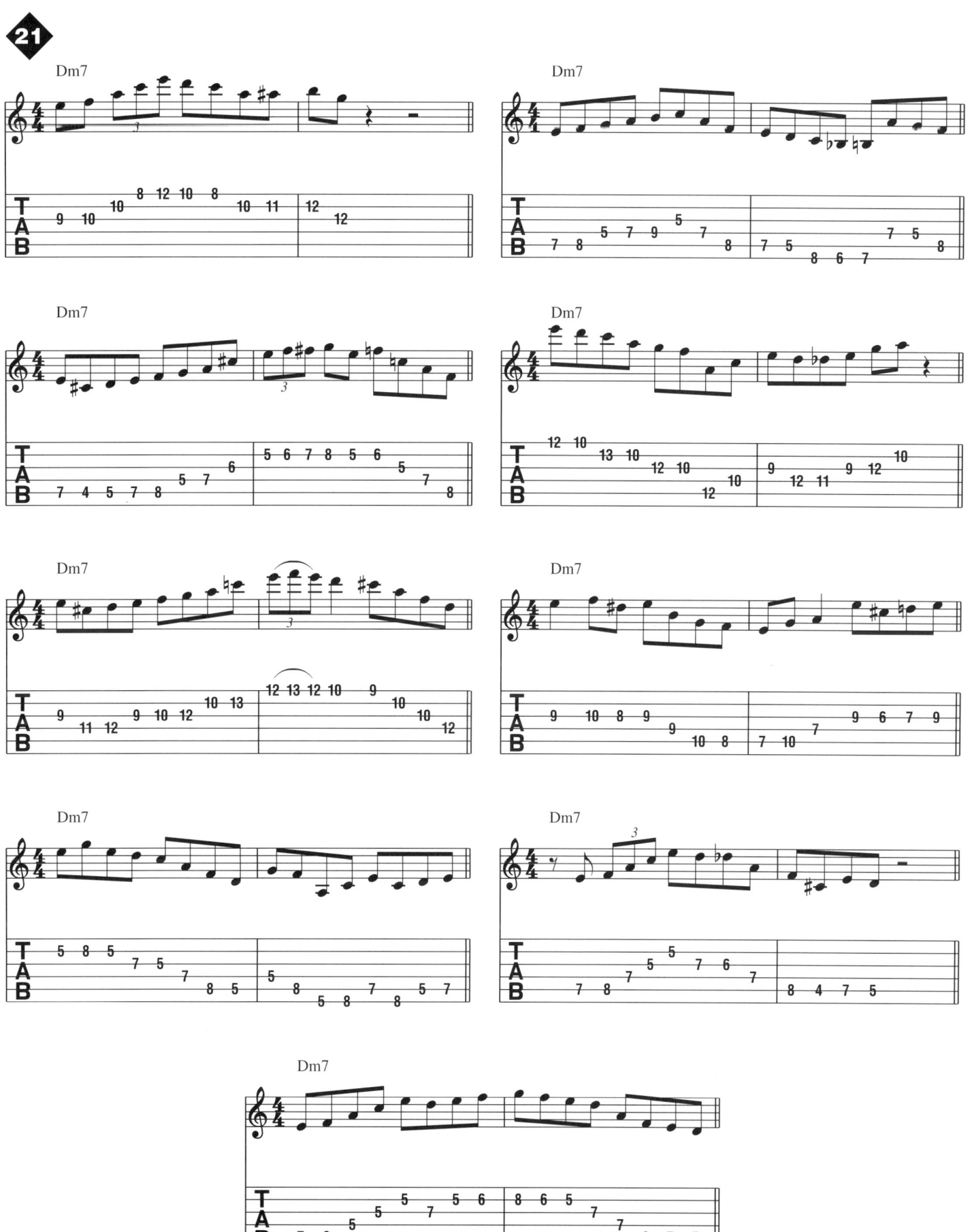

DOMINANT 7TH IDEAS
Starting on the Root

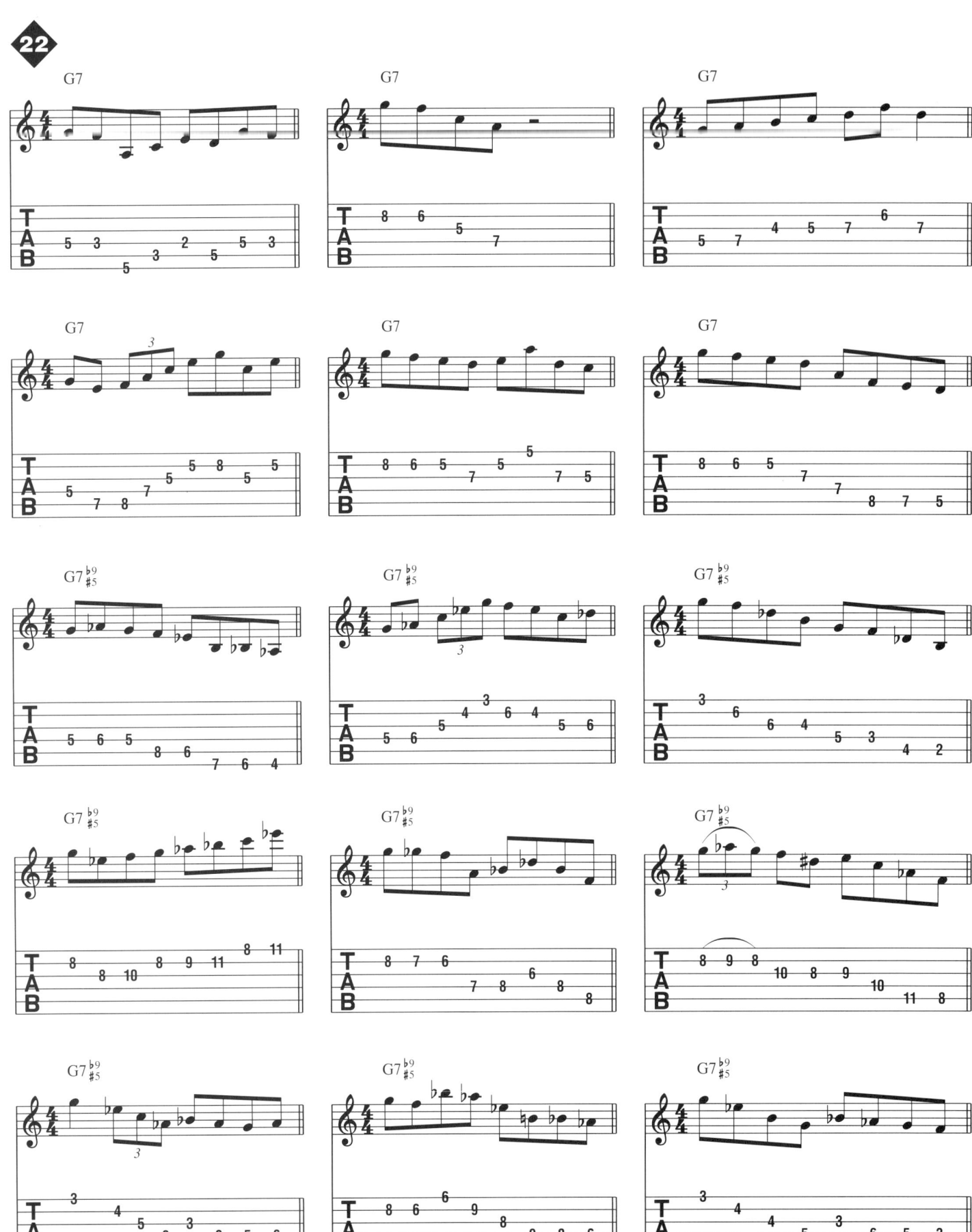

26

Dominant 7th Ideas Starting on the Root

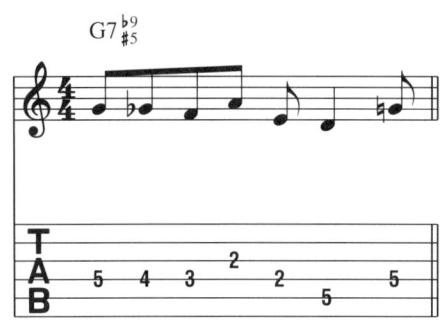
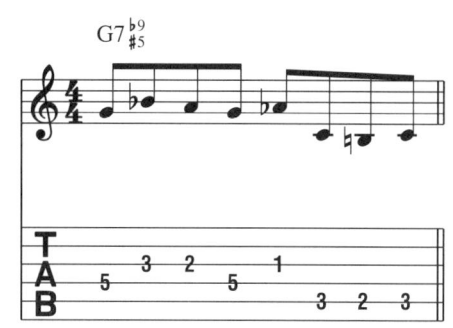

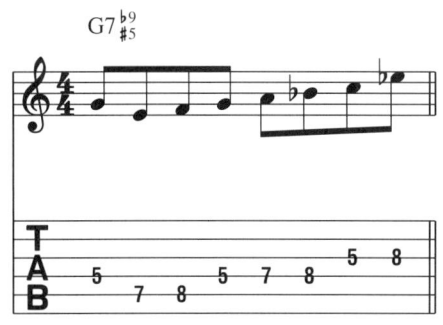
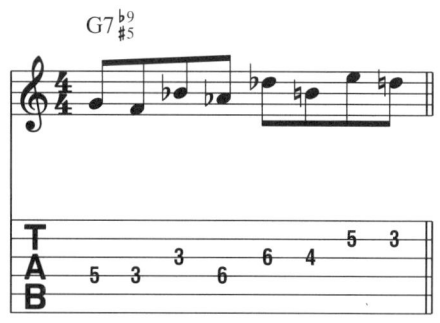
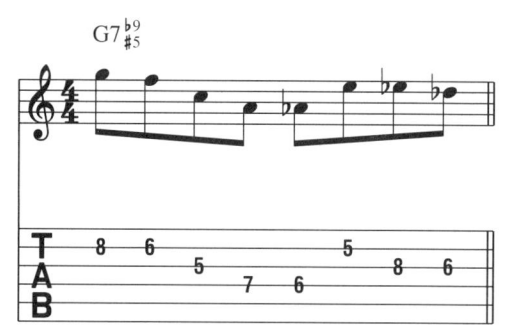

DOMINANT 7TH IDEAS
Starting on the 3rd

23

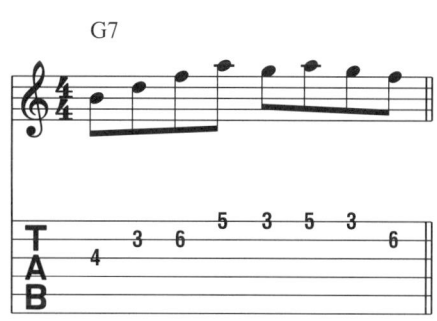
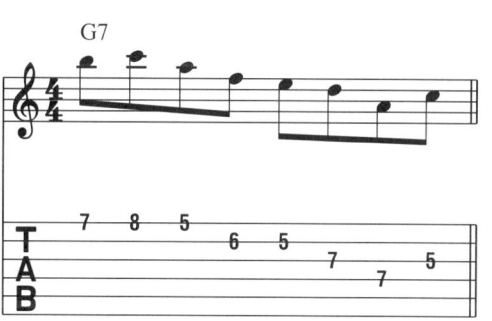

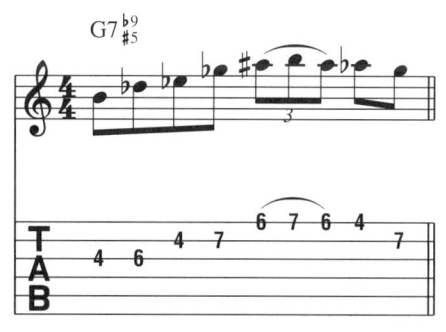
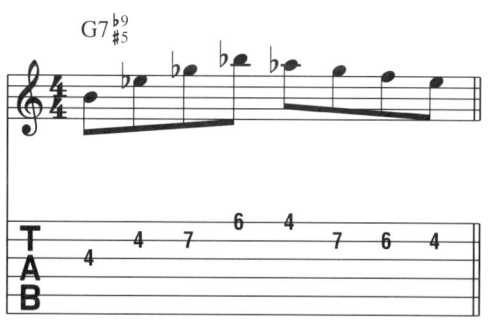

Dominant 7th Ideas Starting on the 3rd

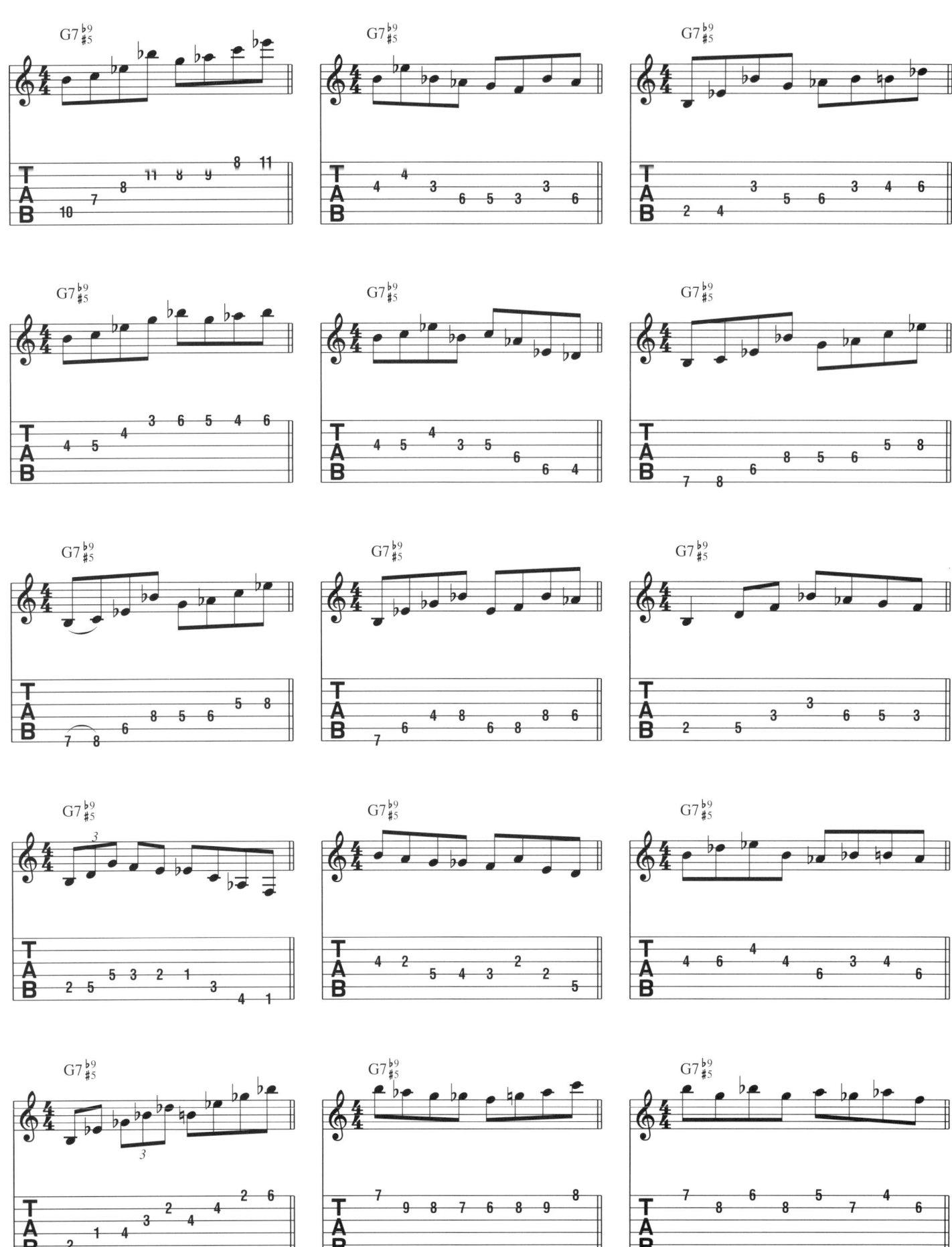

DOMINANT 7TH IDEAS
Starting on the 5th

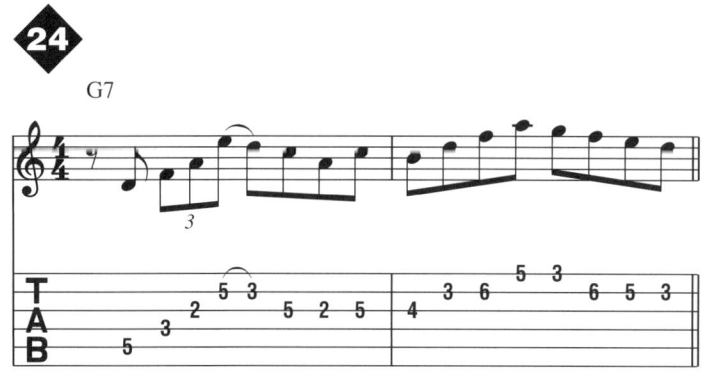

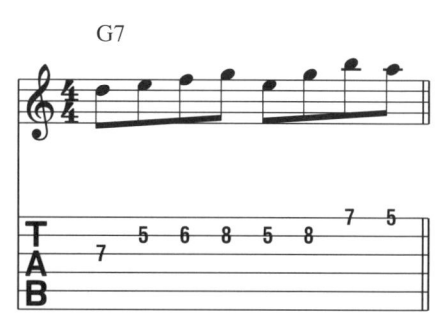

Dominant 7th Ideas Starting on the 5th

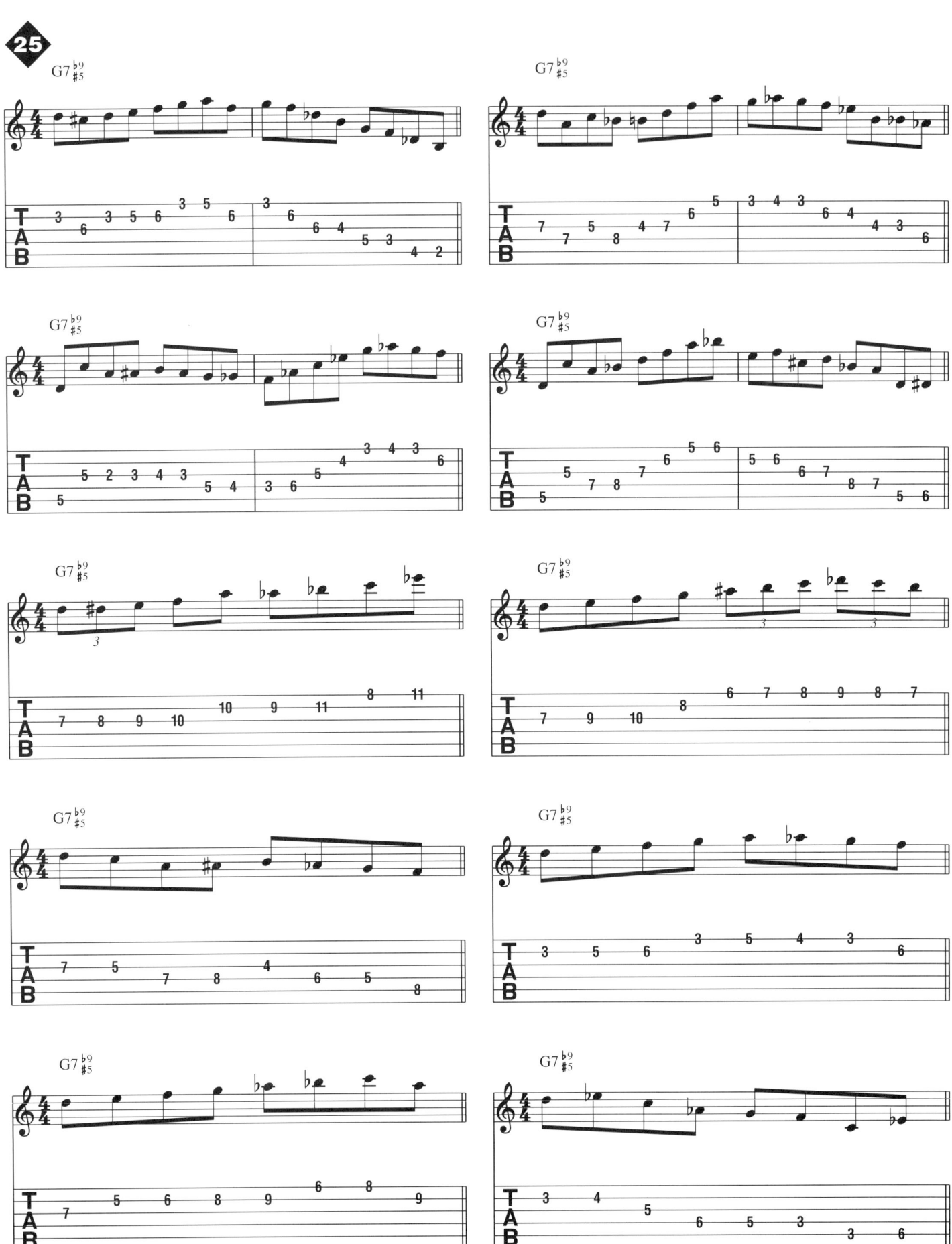

DOMINANT 7TH IDEAS
Starting on the ♭7th

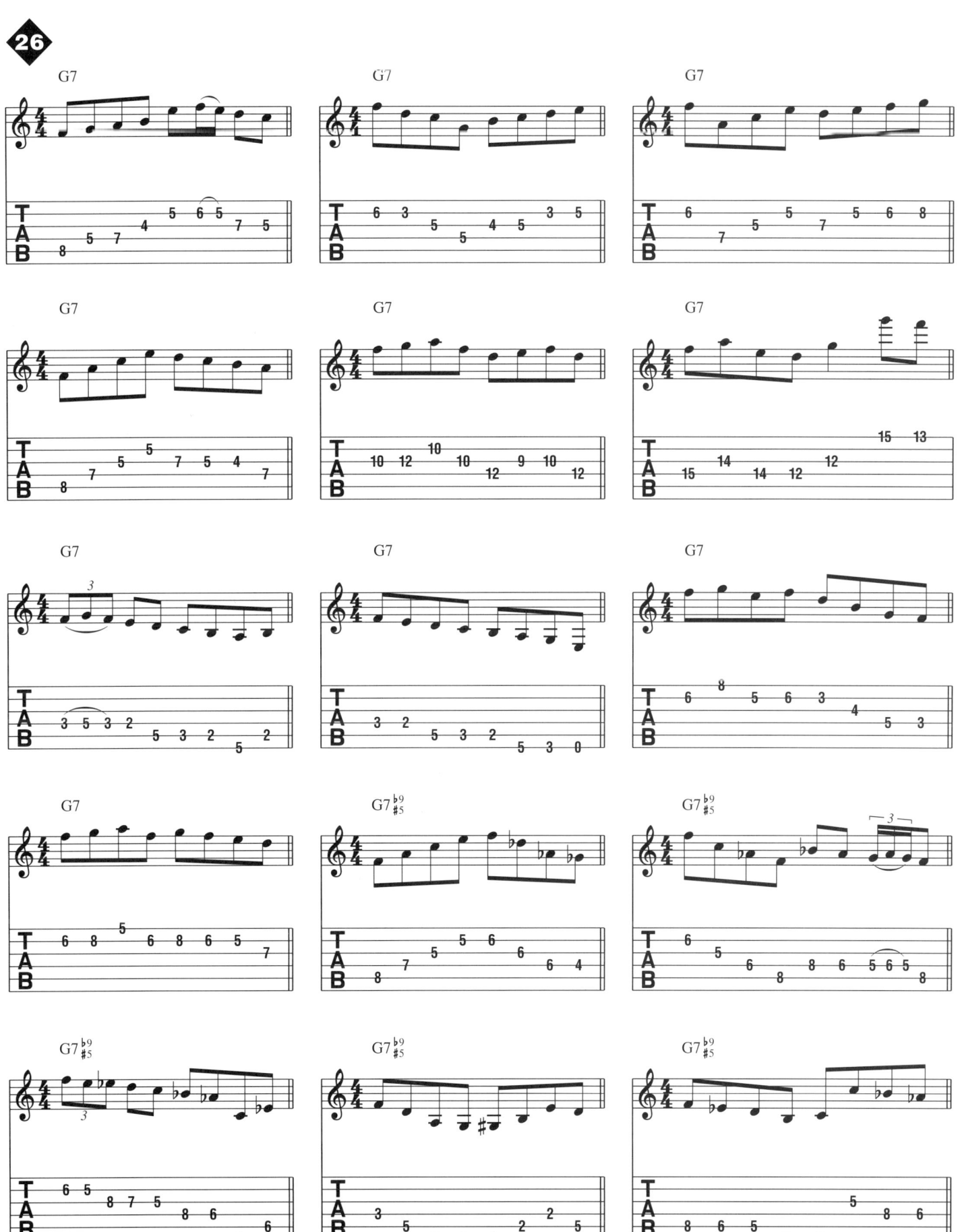

Dominant 7th Ideas Starting on the ♭7th

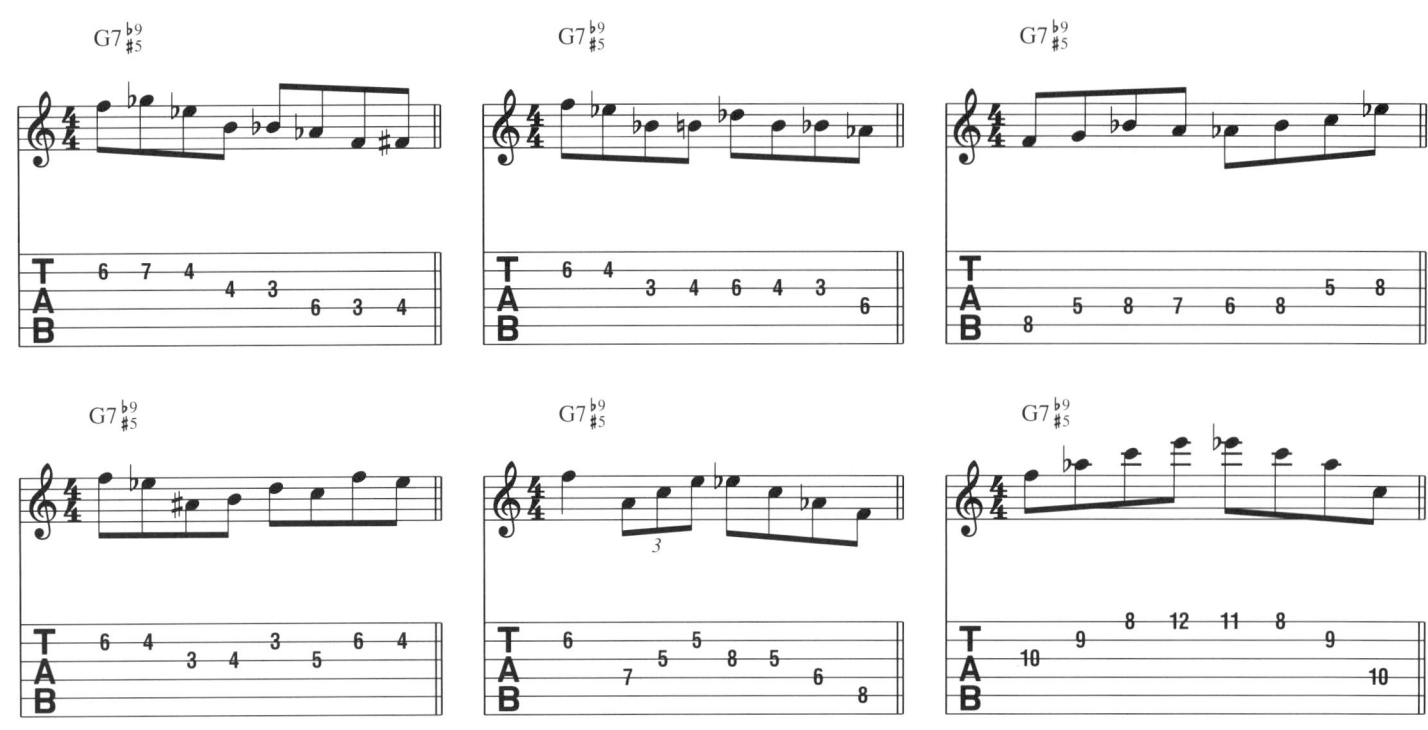

DOMINANT 7TH IDEAS
Starting on the 6th or 13th

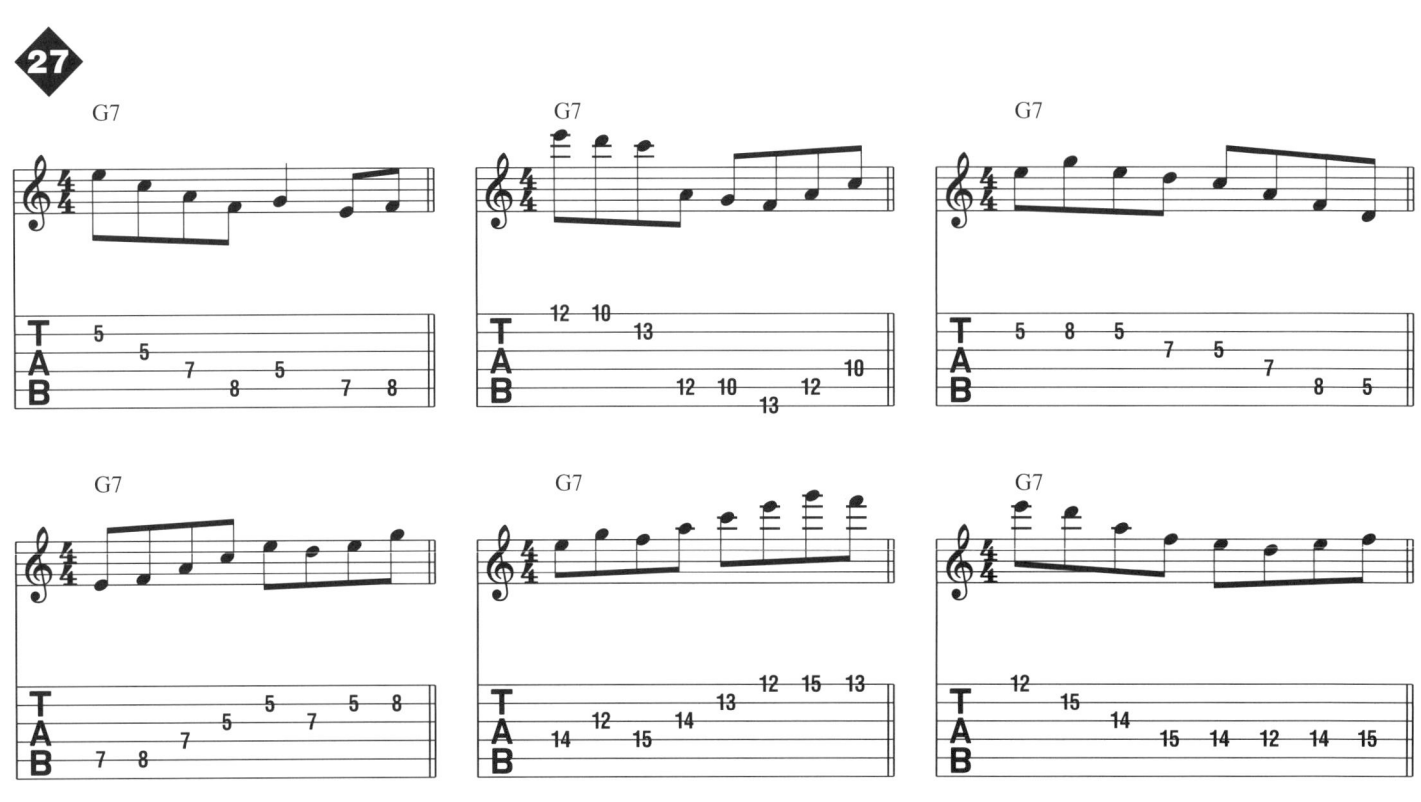

Dominant 7th Ideas Starting on the 6th or 13th

DOMINANT 7TH IDEAS
Starting on the 2nd or 9th

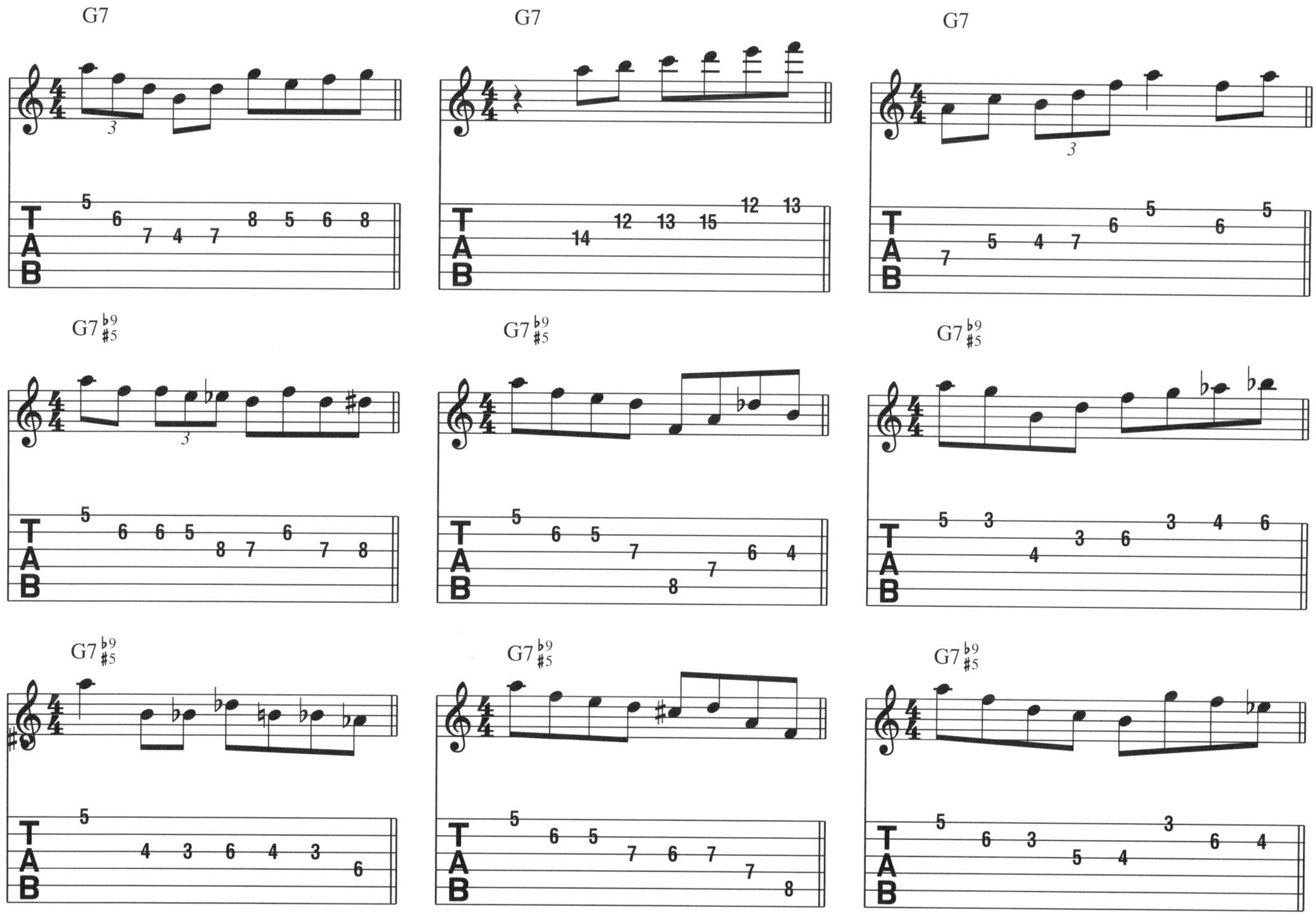

DOMINANT 7TH IDEAS
Starting on the ♭5th

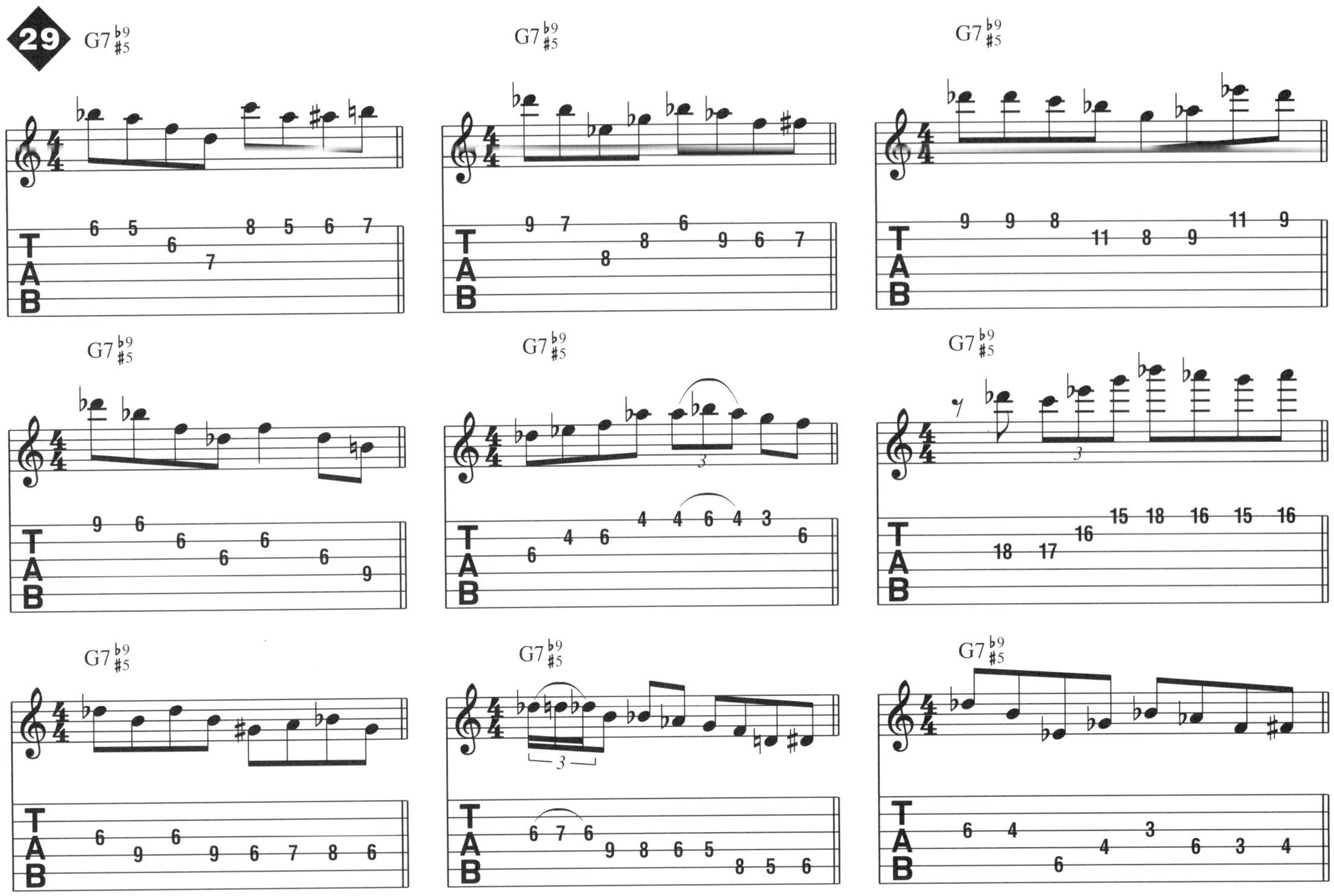

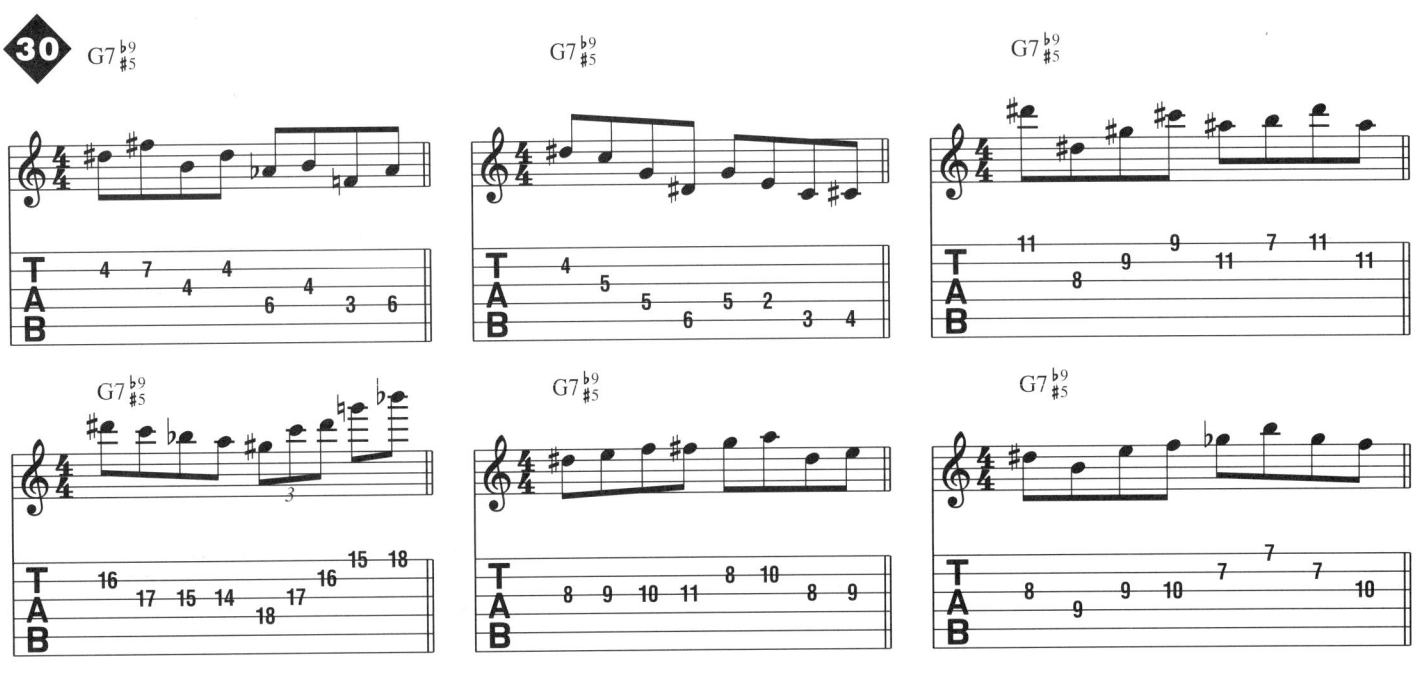

DOMINANT 7TH IDEAS
Starting on the #5th

Dominant 7th Ideas Starting on the #5th

DOMINANT 7TH IDEAS

Starting on the ♭9th

31

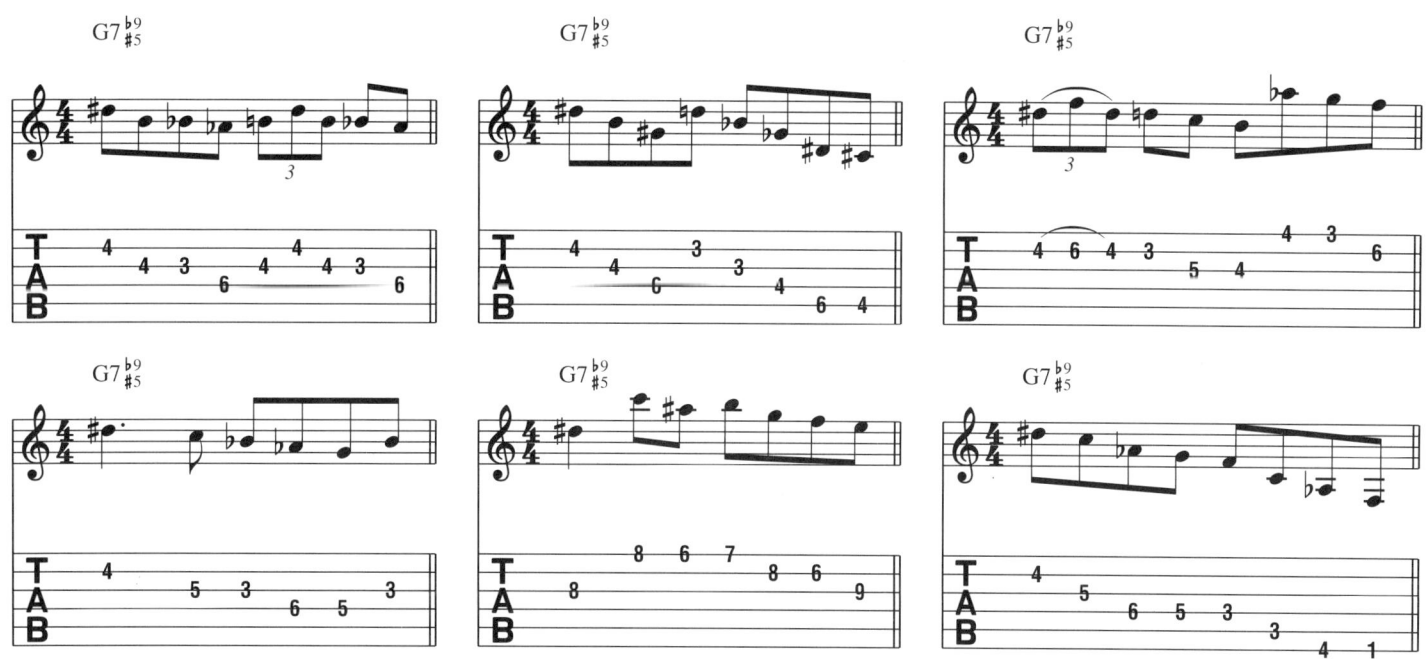

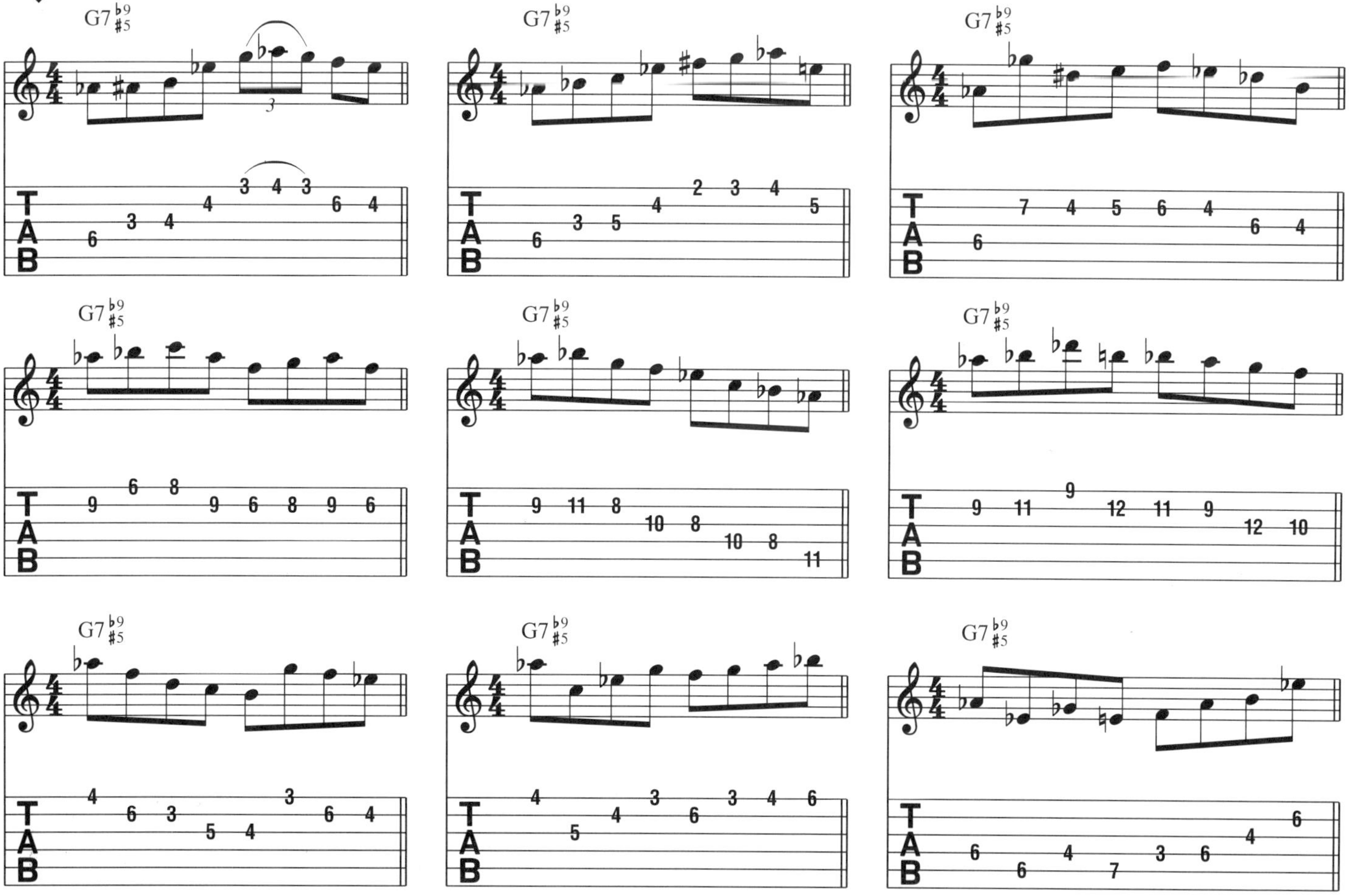

Dominant 7th Ideas
Starting on the ♭9th

32

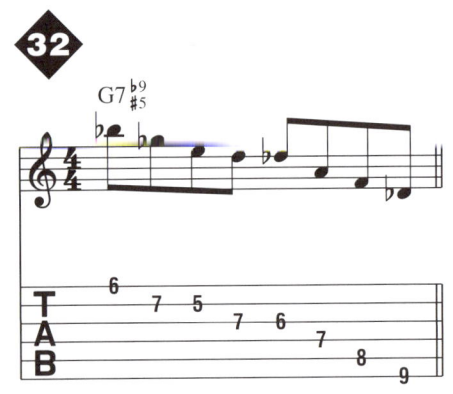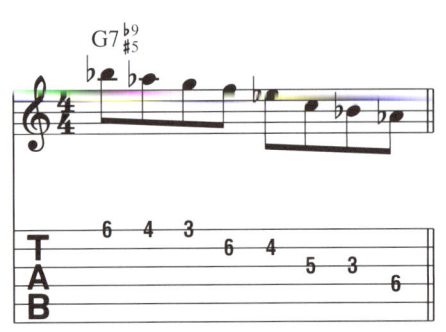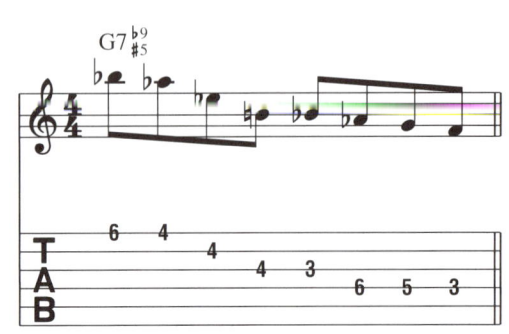
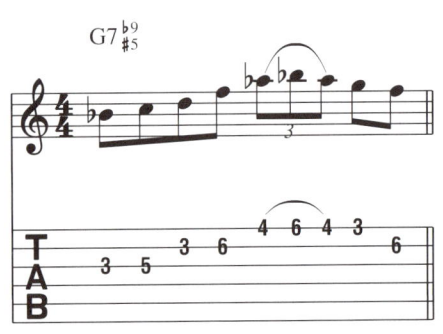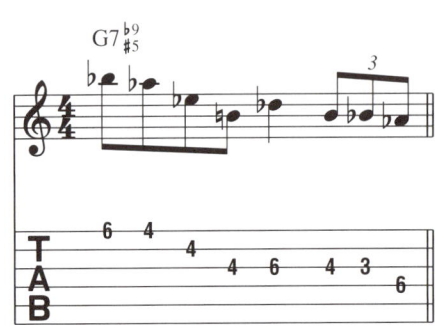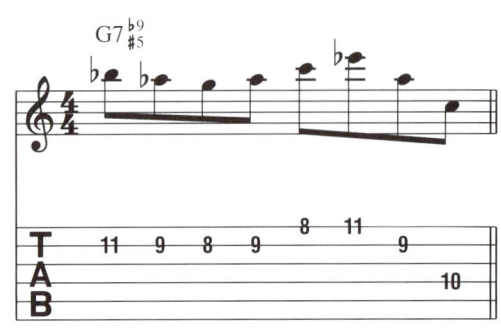
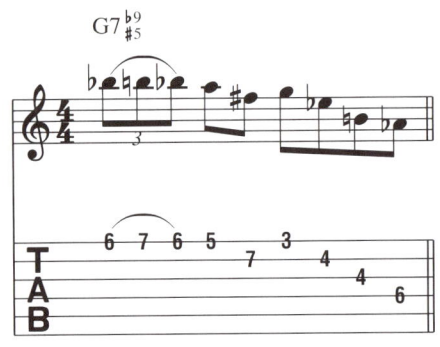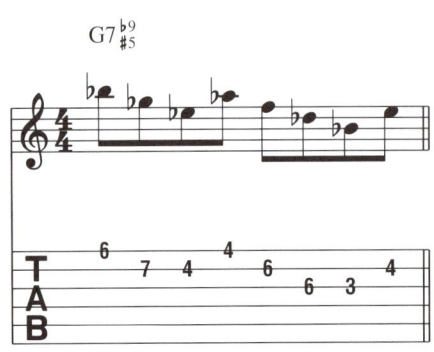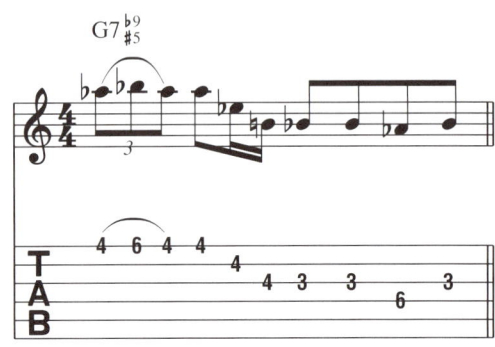
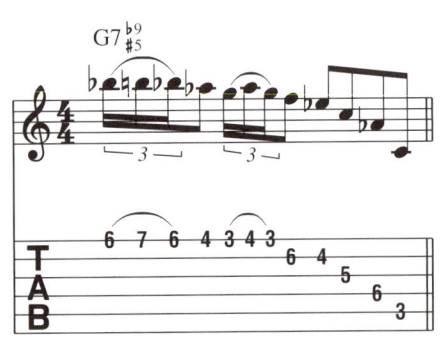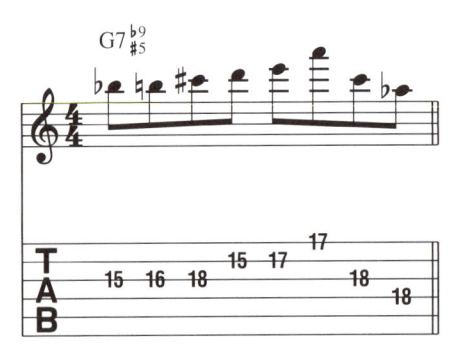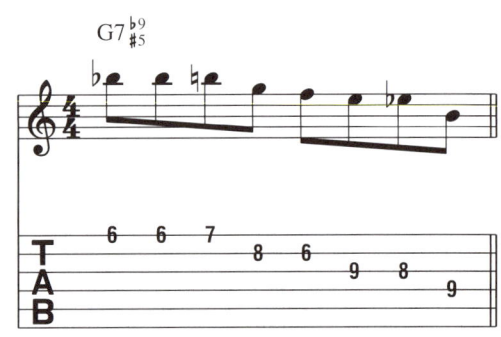

IIm7 V7 Imaj7 IDEAS
Starting on the Root of the IIm7 Chord

IIm7 V7 Imaj7 Starting on the Root of the IIm7 Chord

IIm7 V7 Imaj7 Starting on the Root of the IIm7 Chord

IIm7 V7 Imaj7 Starting on the Root of the IIm7 Chord

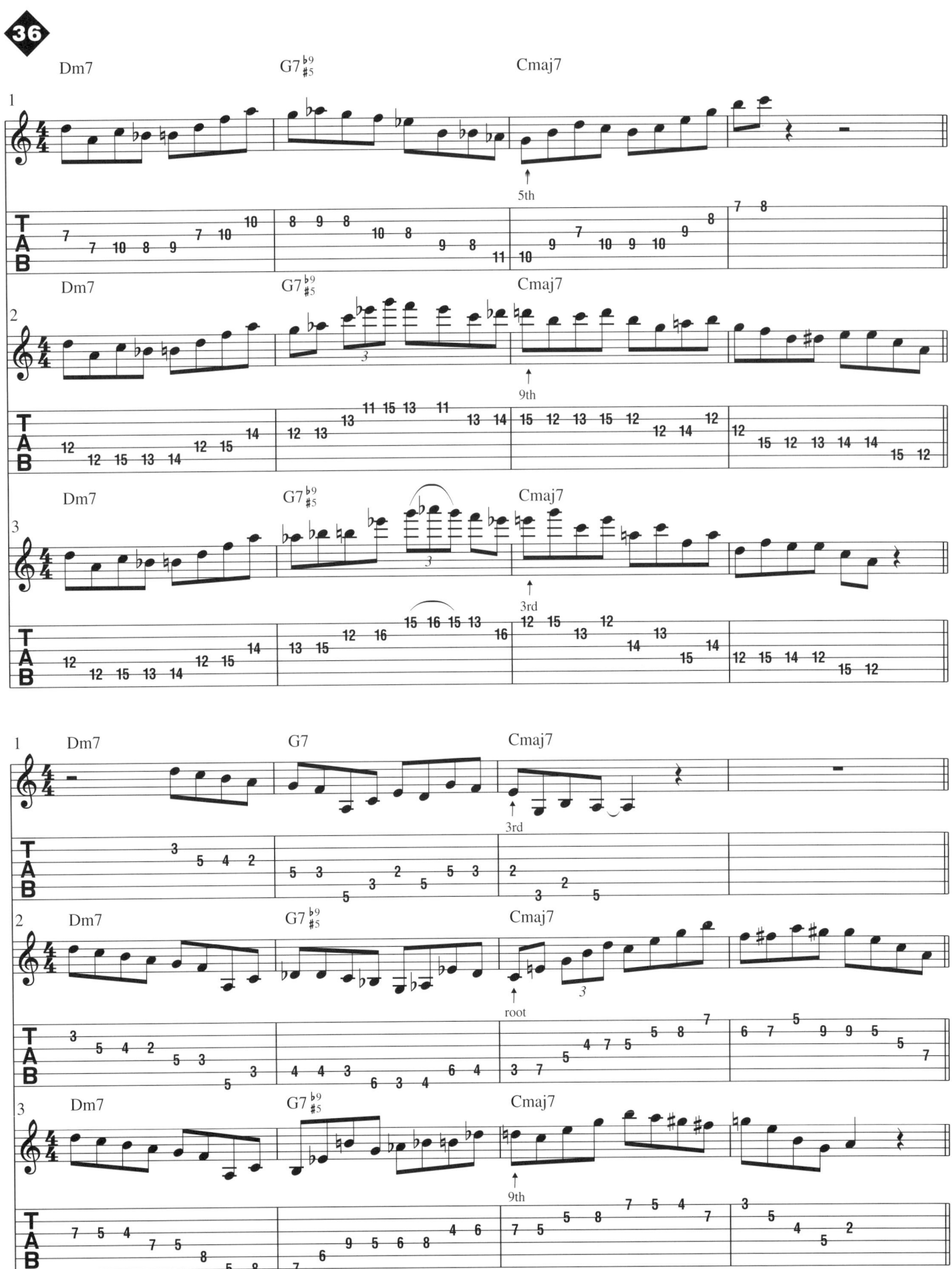

IIm7 V7 Imaj7 Starting on the Root of the IIm7 Chord

IIm7 V7 Imaj7 Starting on the Root of the IIm7 Chord

IIm7 V7 Imaj7 Starting on the Root of the IIm7 Chord

IIm7 V7 Imaj7 Starting on the Root of the IIm7 Chord

IIm7 V7 Imaj7 Starting on the Root of the IIm7 Chord

IIm7 V7 Imaj7 Starting on the Root of the IIm7 Chord

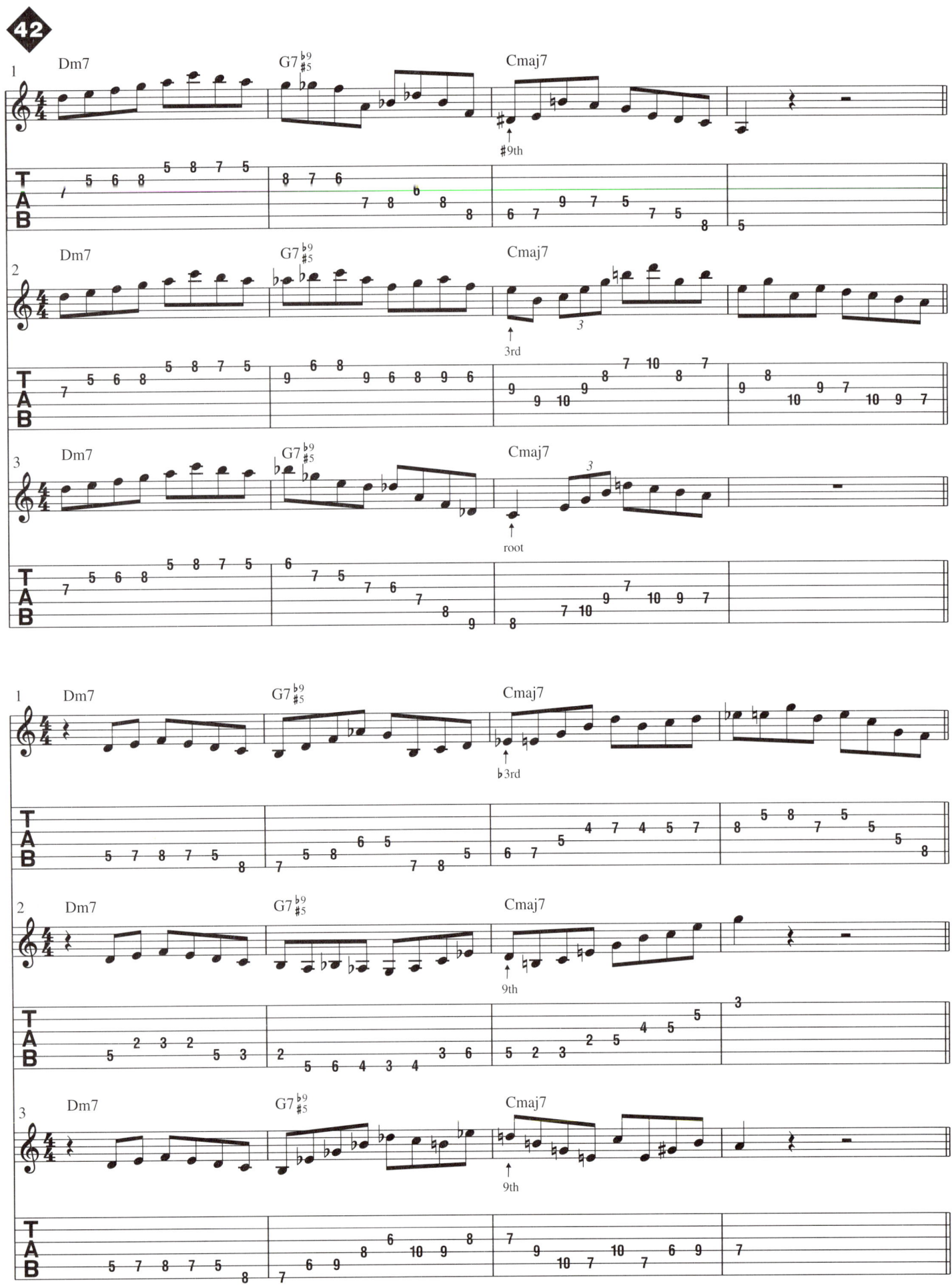

IIm7 V7 Imaj7 Starting on the Root of the IIm7 Chord

IIm7 V7 Imaj7 Starting on the Root of the IIm7 Chord

IIm7 V7 Imaj7 Starting on the Root of the IIm7 Chord

IIm7 V7 Imaj7 Starting on the Root of the IIm7 Chord

IIm7 V7 Imaj7 Starting on the Root of the IIm7 Chord

IIm7 V7 Imaj7 IDEAS
Starting on the ♭3rd of the IIm7 Chord

IIm7 V7 Imaj7 Starting on the ♭3rd of the IIm7 Chord

IIm7 V7 Imaj7 Starting on the ♭3rd of the IIm7 Chord

IIm7 V7 Imaj7 Starting on the ♭3rd of the IIm7 Chord

IIm7 V7 Imaj7 Starting on the ♭3rd of the IIm7 Chord

IIm7 V7 Imaj7 Starting on the ♭3rd of the IIm7 Chord

IIm7 V7 Imaj7 Starting on the ♭3rd of the IIm7 Chord

IIm7 V7 Imaj7 Starting on the ♭3rd of the IIm7 Chord

IIm7 V7 Imaj7 Starting on the ♭3rd of the IIm7 Chord

IIm7 V7 Imaj7 Starting on the ♭3rd of the IIm7 Chord

IIm7 V7 Imaj7 Starting on the ♭3rd of the IIm7 Chord

IIm7 V7 Imaj7 Starting on the ♭3rd of the IIm7 Chord

IIm7 V7 Imaj7 Starting on the ♭3rd of the IIm7 Chord

IIm7 V7 Imaj7 Starting on the ♭3rd of the IIm7 Chord

IIm7 V7 Imaj7 Starting on the ♭3rd of the IIm7 Chord

IIm7 V7 Imaj7 Starting on the ♭3rd of the IIm7 Chord

IIm7 V7 Imaj7 IDEAS
Starting on the 4th or 11th of the IIm7 Chord

IIm7 V7 Imaj7 Starting on the 4th or 11th of the IIm7 Chord

IIm7 V7 Imaj7 Starting on the 4th or 11th of the IIm7 Chord

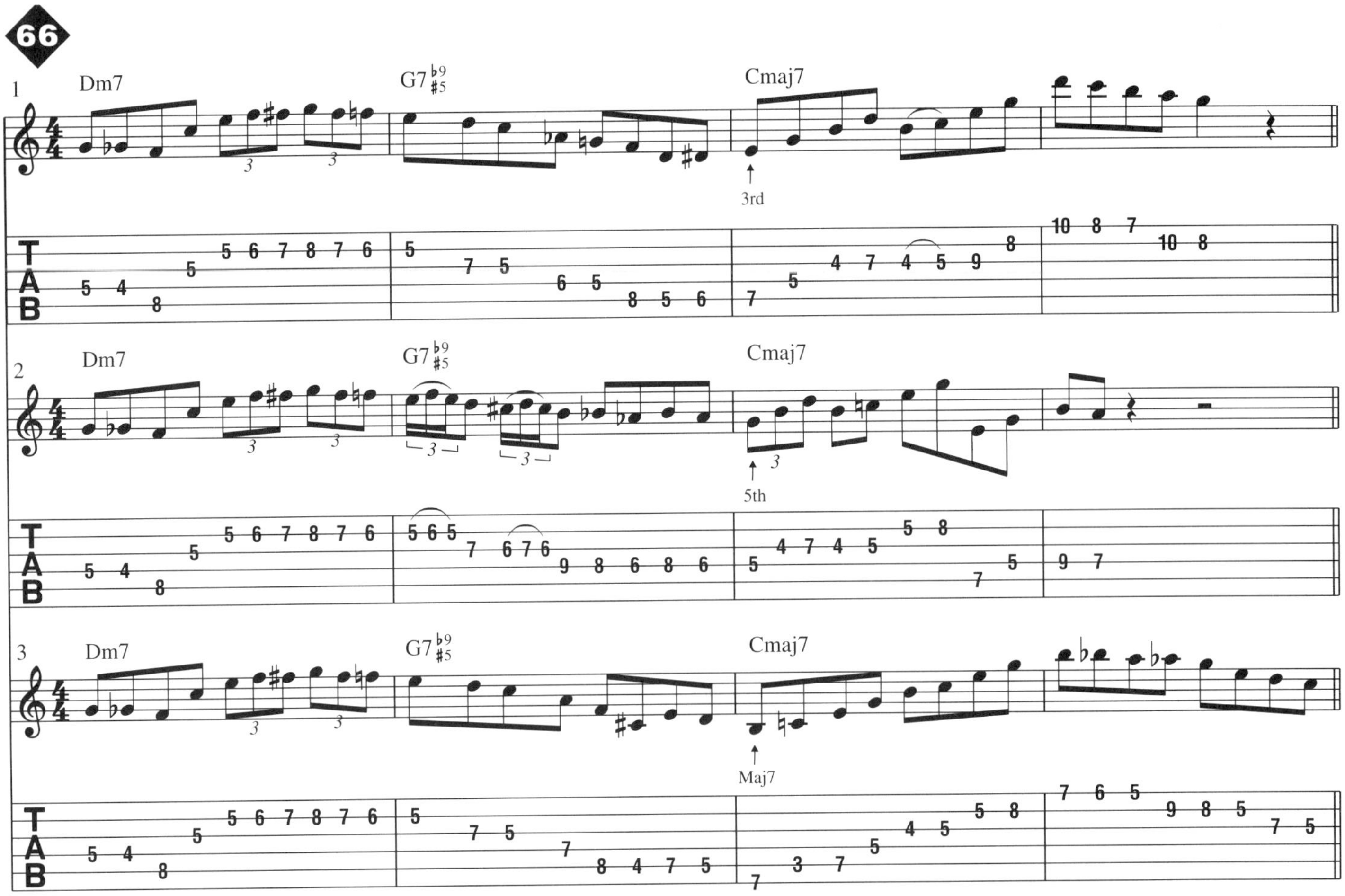

IIm7 V7 Imaj7 Starting on the 4th or 11th of the IIm7 Chord

IIm7 V7 Imaj7
Starting on the 5th of the IIm7 Chord

IIm7 V7 Imaj7 Starting on the 5th of the IIm7 Chord

IIm7 V7 Imaj7 Starting on the 5th of the IIm7 Chord

IIm7 V7 Imaj7 Starting on the 5th of the IIm7 Chord

IIm7 V7 Imaj7 Starting on the 5th of the IIm7 Chord

IIm7 V7 Imaj7 Starting on the 5th of the IIm7 Chord

IIm7 V7 Imaj7 Starting on the 5th of the IIm7 Chord

IIm7 V7 Imaj7 IDEAS
Starting on the 6th or 13th of the IIm7 Chord

IIm7 V7 Imaj7 Starting on the 6th or 13th of the IIm7 Chord

IIm7 V7 Imaj7 IDEAS
Starting on the ♭7th of the IIm7 Chord

IIm7 V7 Imaj7 IDEAS
Starting on the 2nd or 9th of the IIm7 Chord

IIm7 V7 Imaj7 Starting on the 2nd or 9th of the IIm7 Chord

IIm7 V7 Imaj7 Starting on the 2nd or 9th of the IIm7 Chord

IIm7 V7 Imaj7 Starting on the 2nd or 9th of the IIm7 Chord

IIm7 V7 Imaj7 Starting on the 2nd or 9th of the IIm7 Chord

IIm7 V7 Imaj7 Starting on the 2nd or 9th of the IIm7 Chord

IIm7 V7 Imaj7 Starting on the 2nd or 9th of the IIm7 Chord

IIm7 V7 Imaj7 Starting on the 2nd or 9th of the IIm7 Chord

IIm7 V7 IDEAS
Starting on the Root of the IIm7 Chord

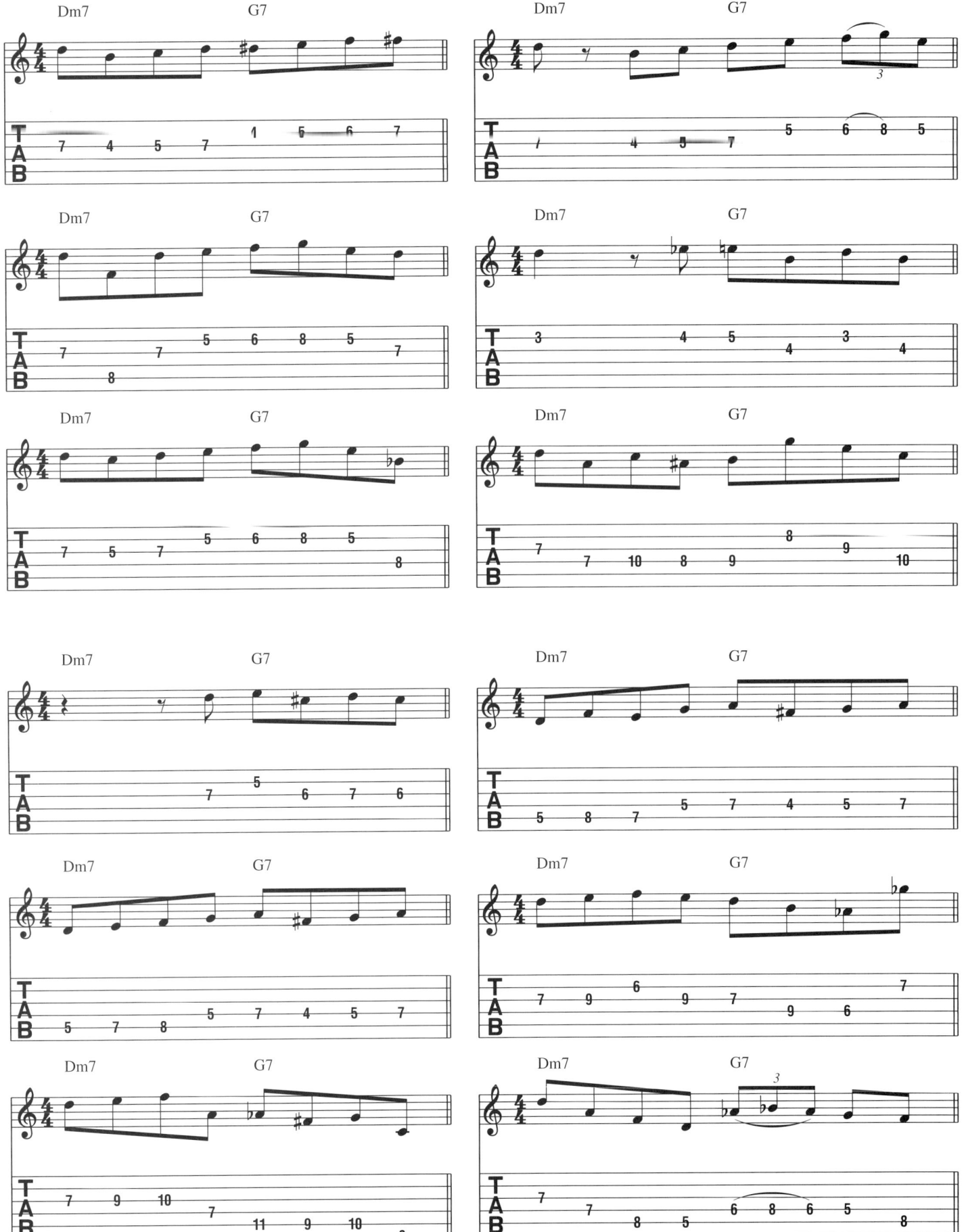

IIm7 V7 Starting on the Root of the IIm7 Chord

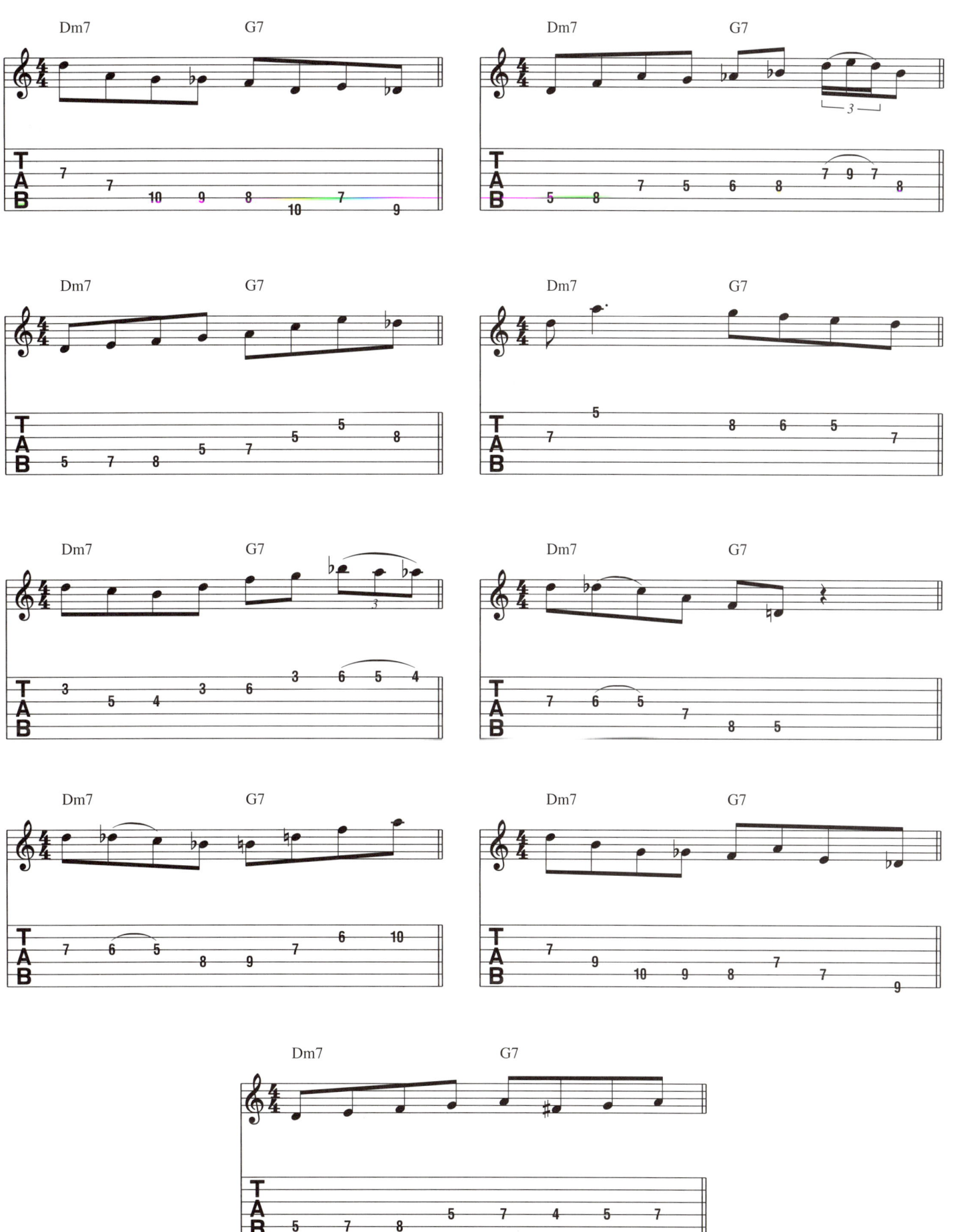

IIm7 V7 IDEAS
Starting on the ♭3rd of the IIm7 Chord

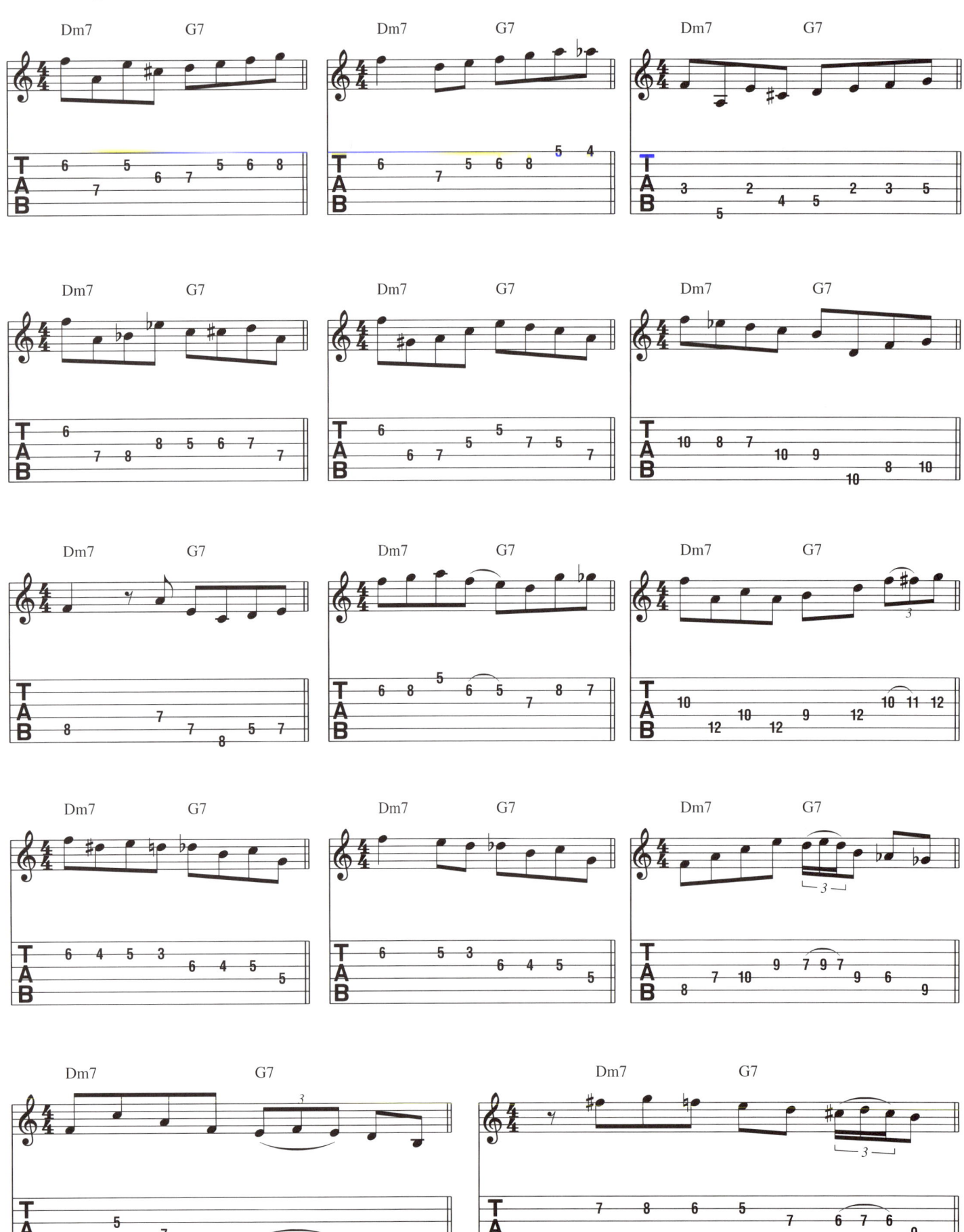

IIm7 V7 IDEAS
Starting on the 4th or 11th of the IIm7 Chord

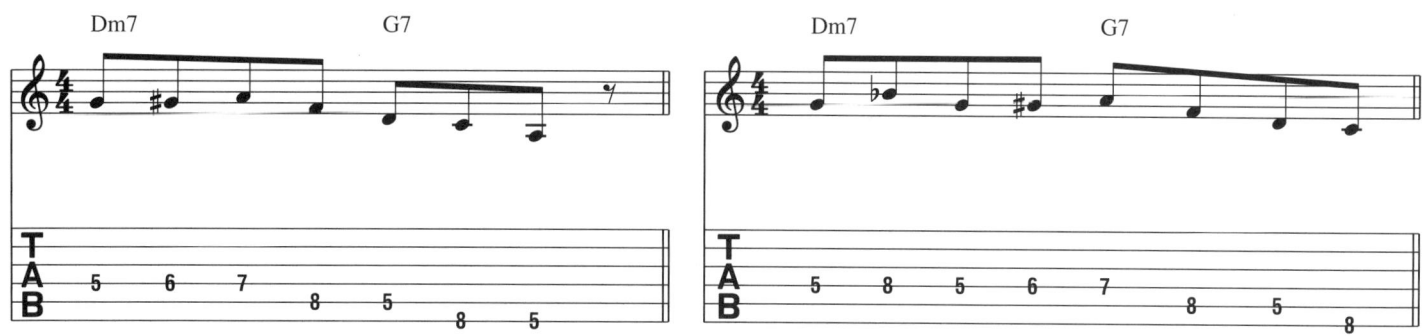

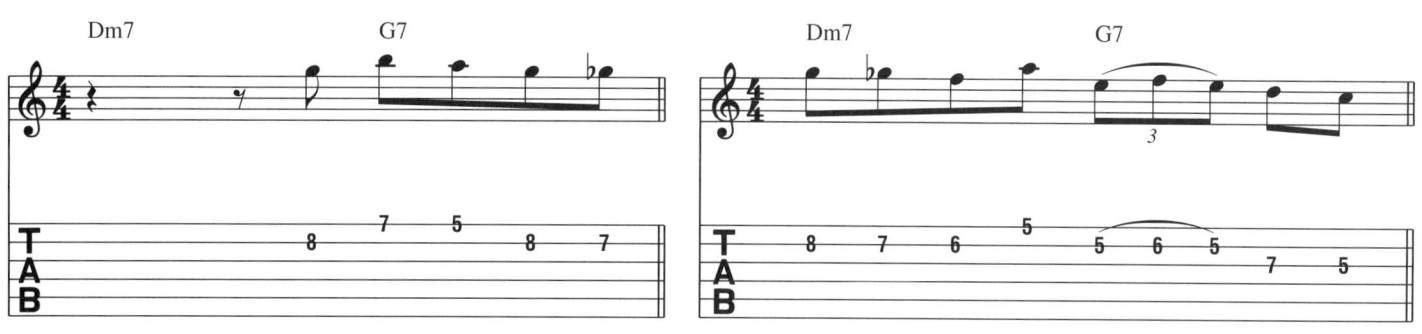

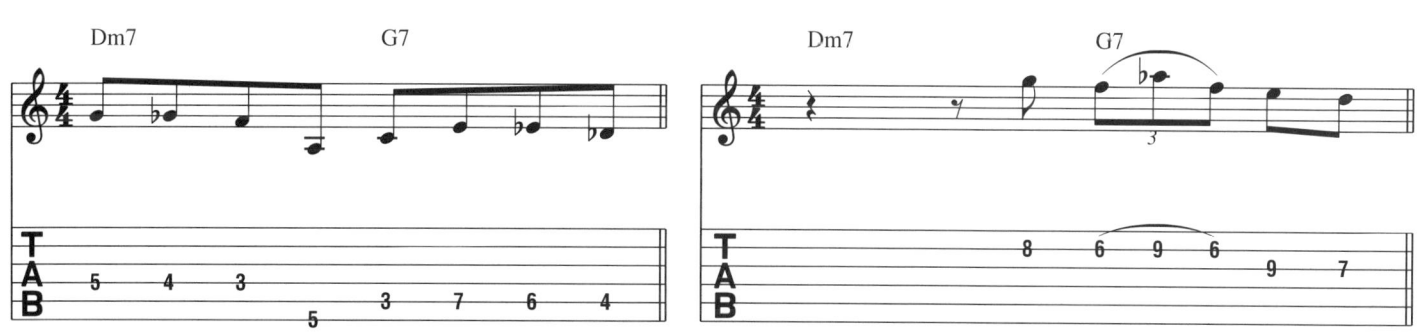

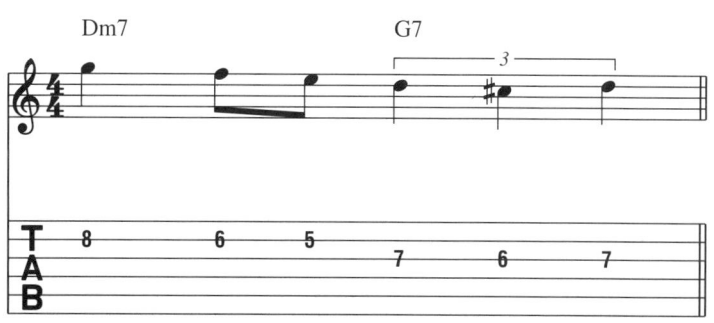

IIm7 V7 IDEAS
Starting on the 5th of the IIm7 Chord

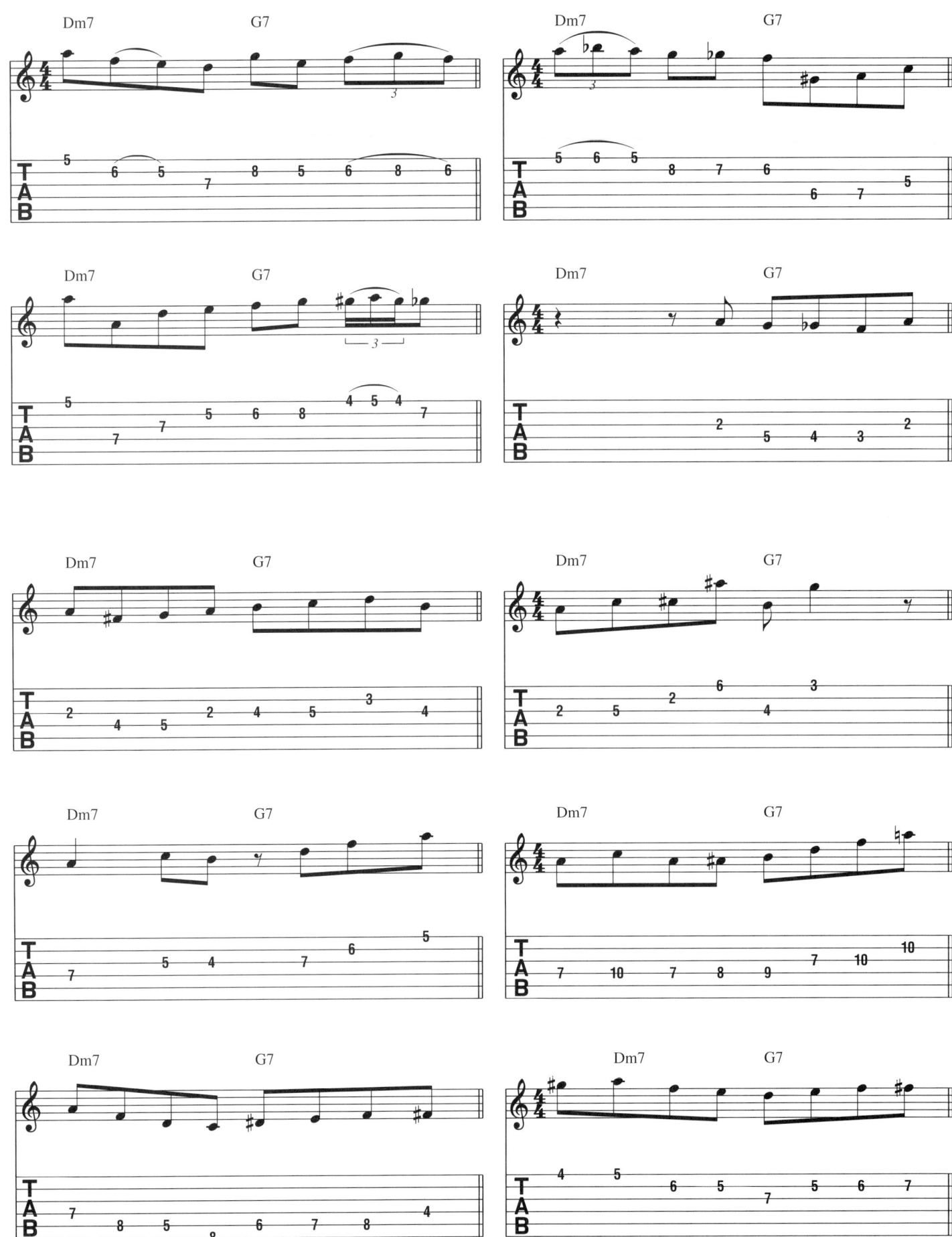

IIm7 V7 IDEAS
Starting on the 6th or 13th of the IIm7 Chord

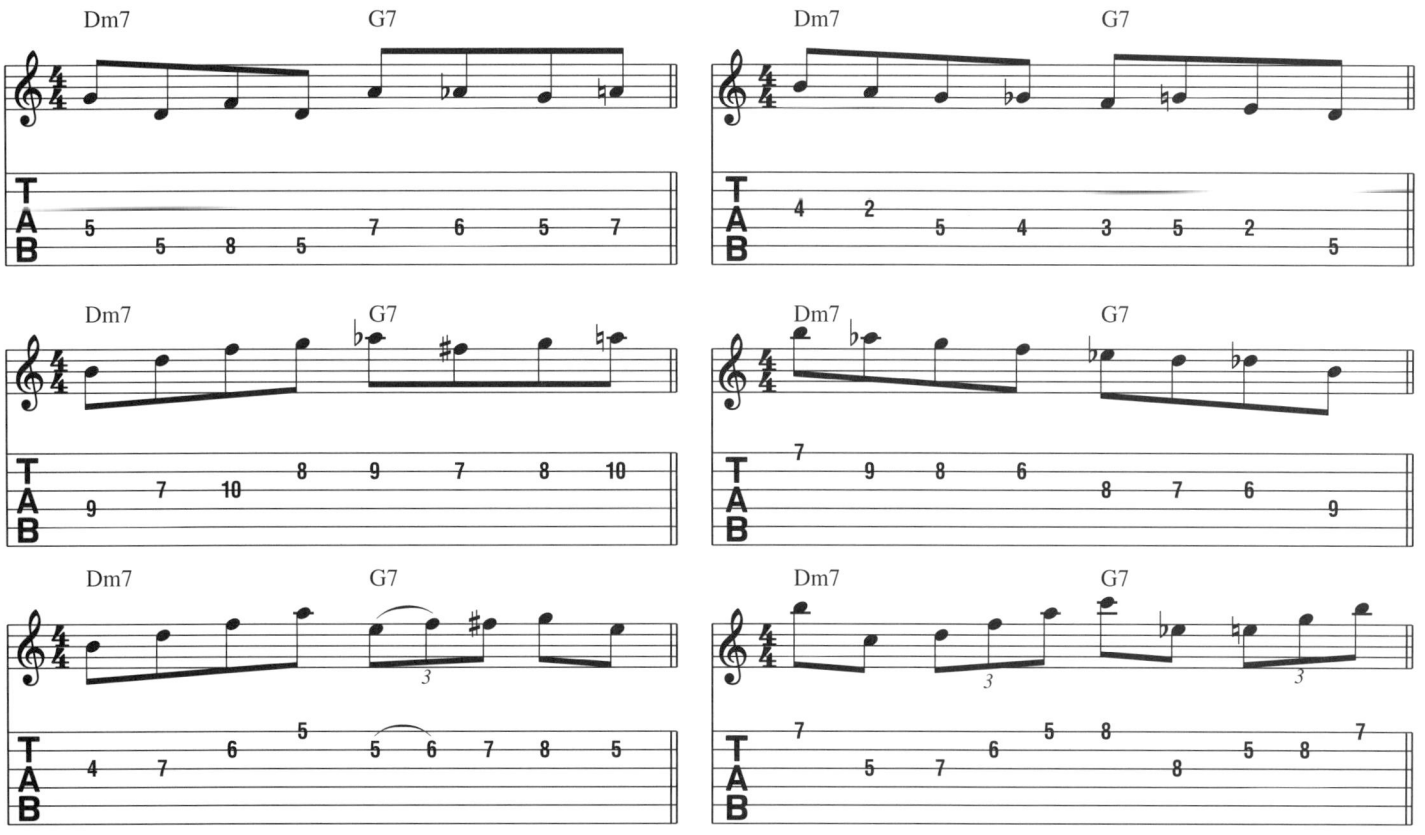

IIm7 V7 IDEAS
Starting on the ♭7th of the IIm7 Chord

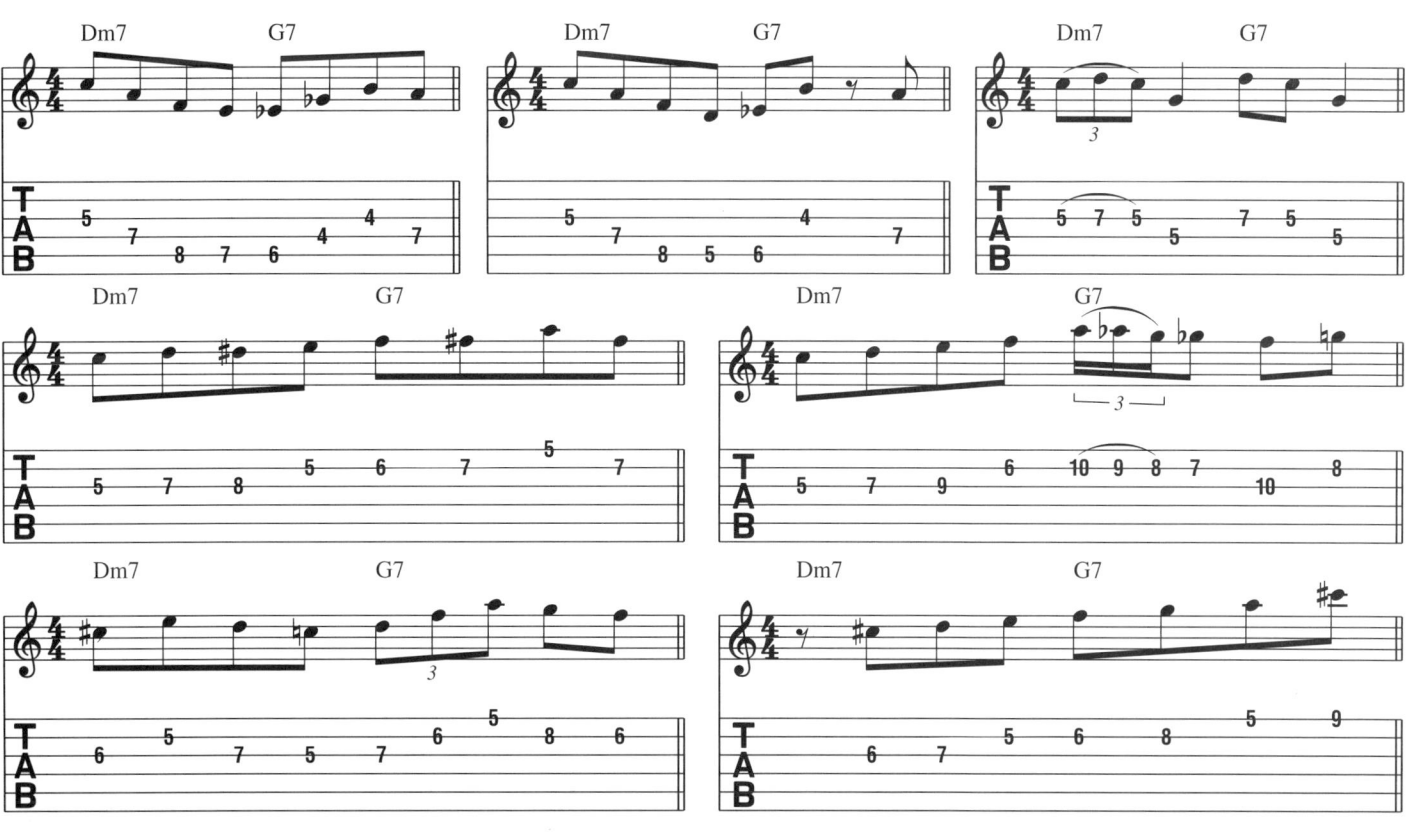

IIm7 V7 IDEAS
Starting on the 2nd or 9th of the IIm7 Chord

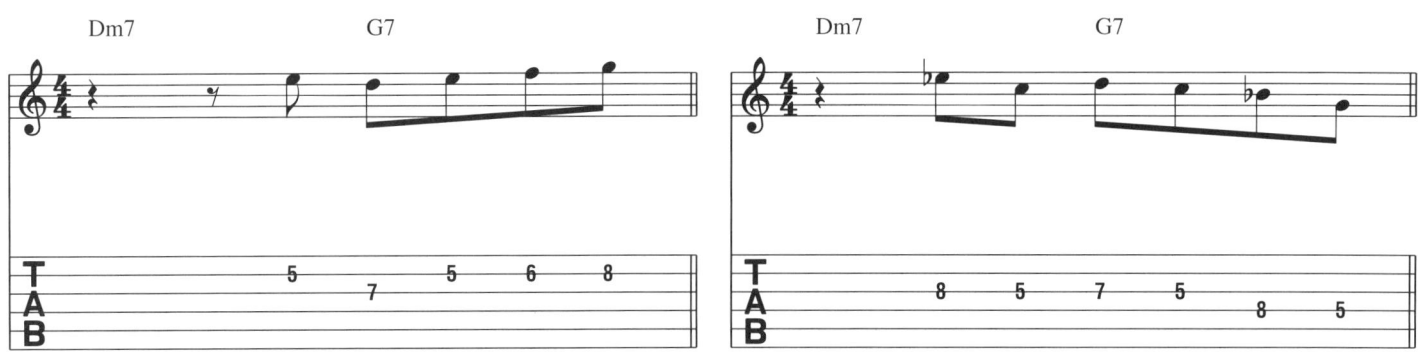

TURNAROUNDS
Starting on the Root of the Imaj7 Chord

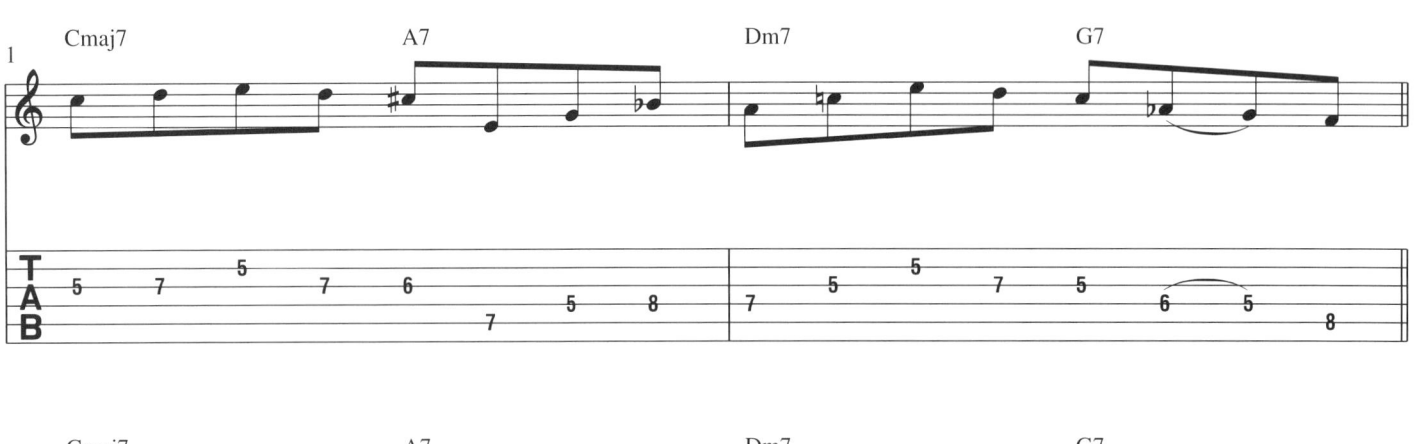

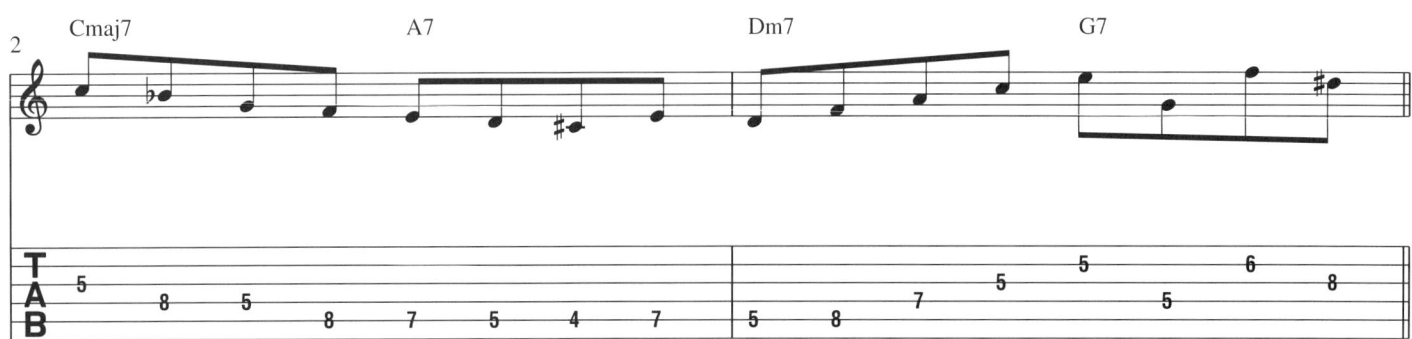

Turnarounds Starting on the Root of the Imaj7 Chord

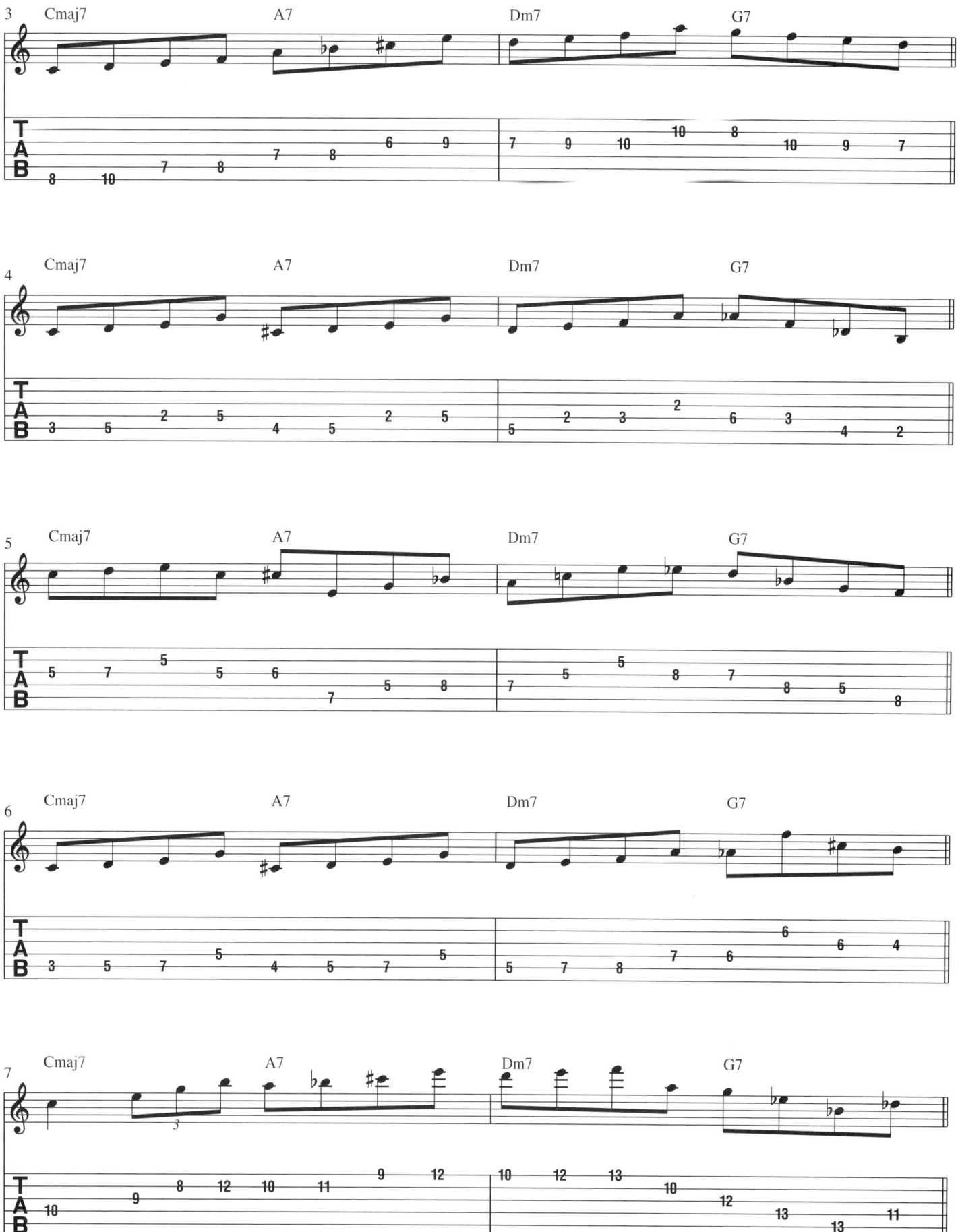

TURNAROUNDS
Starting on the 3rd of the Imaj7 Chord

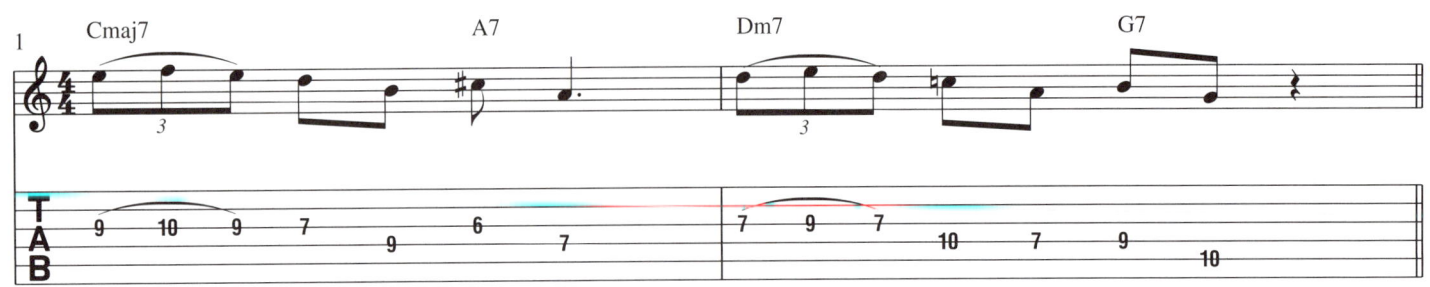

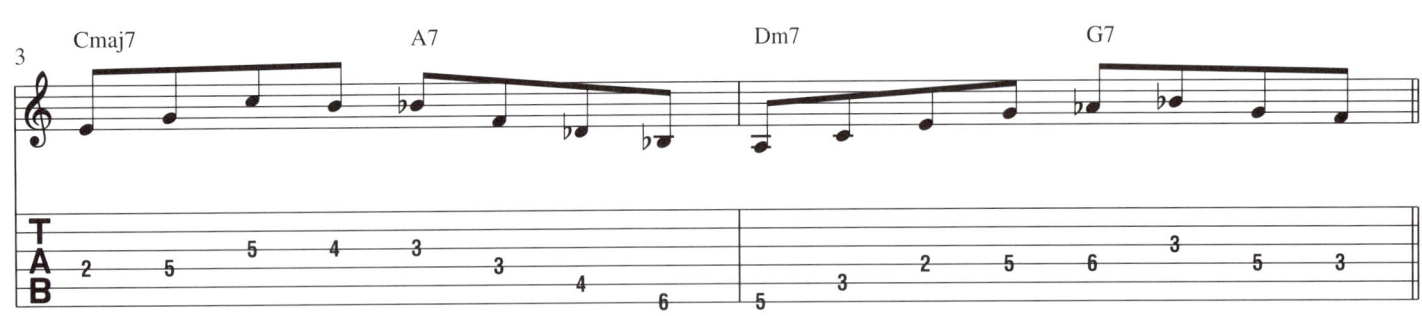

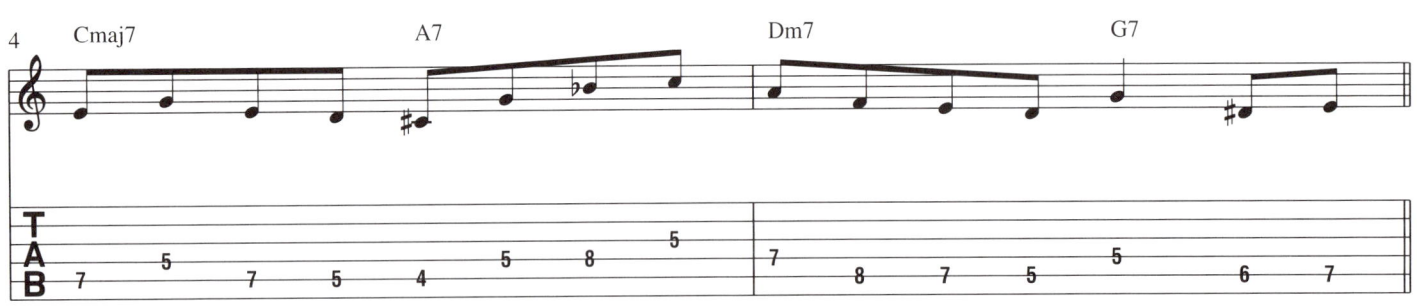

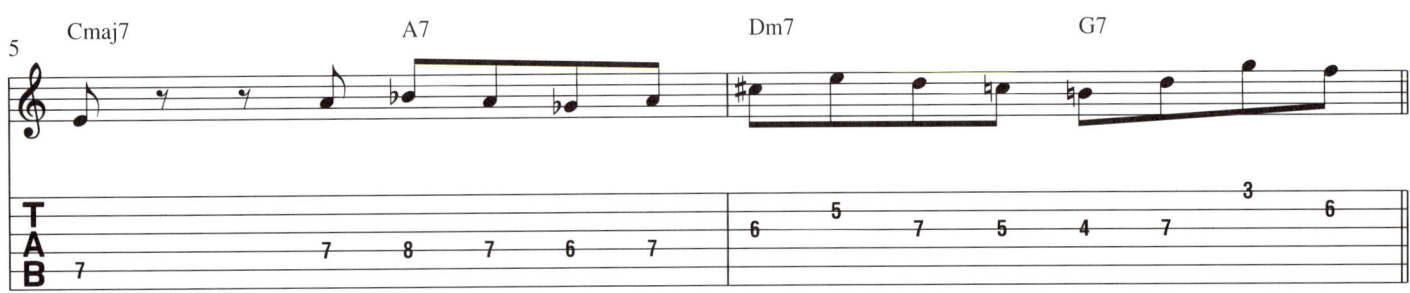

Turnarounds Starting on the 3rd of the Imaj7 Chord

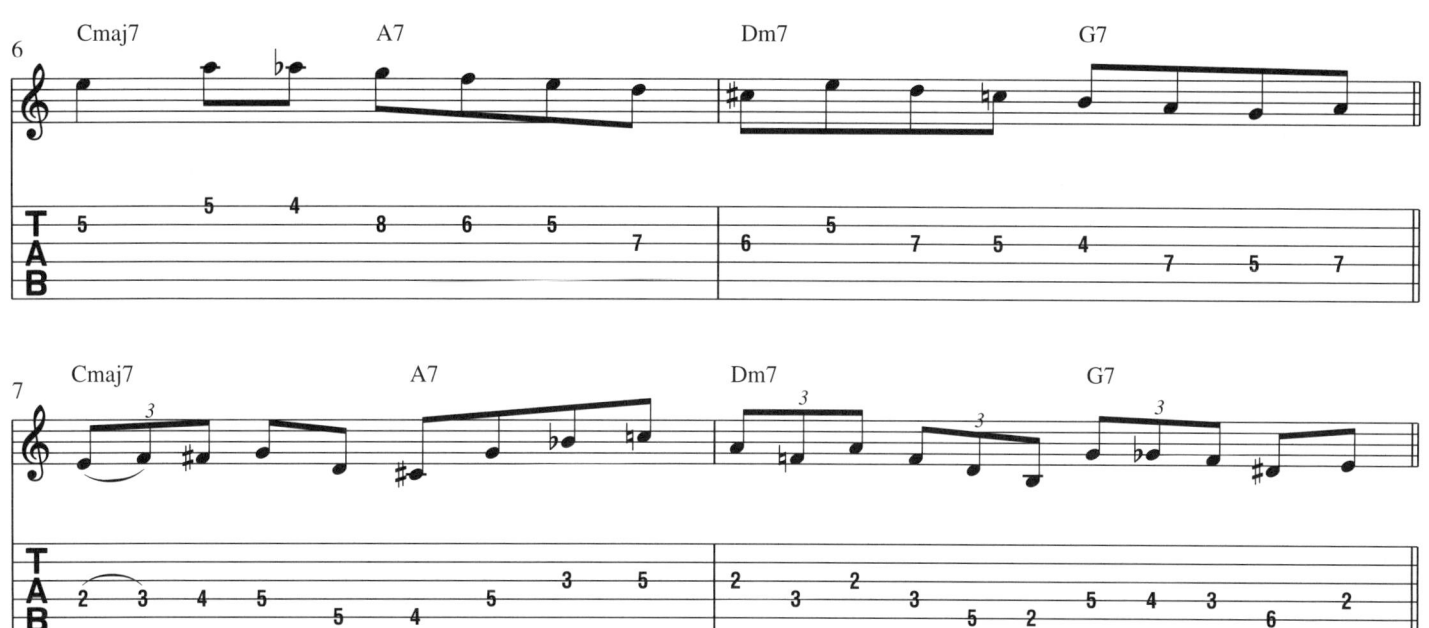

6

7

TURNAROUNDS

Starting on the 5th of the Imaj7 Chord

1

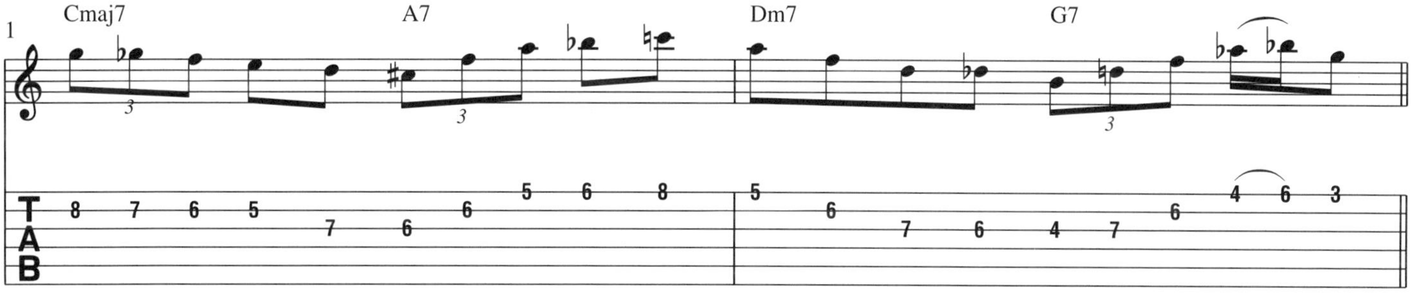

2

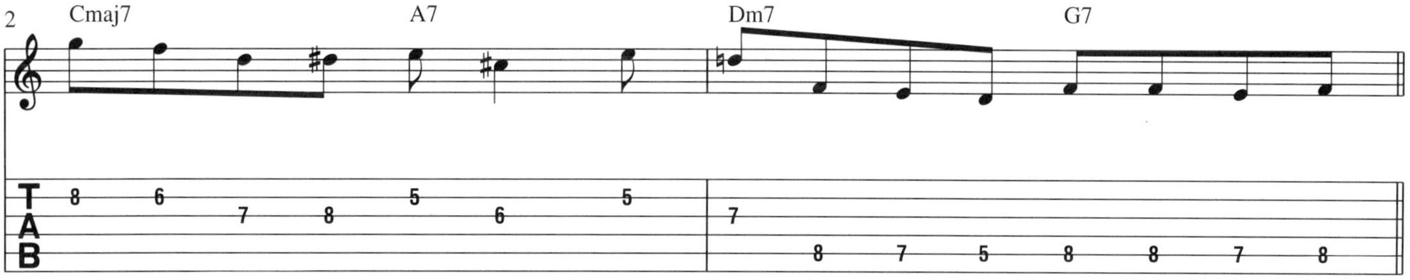

3

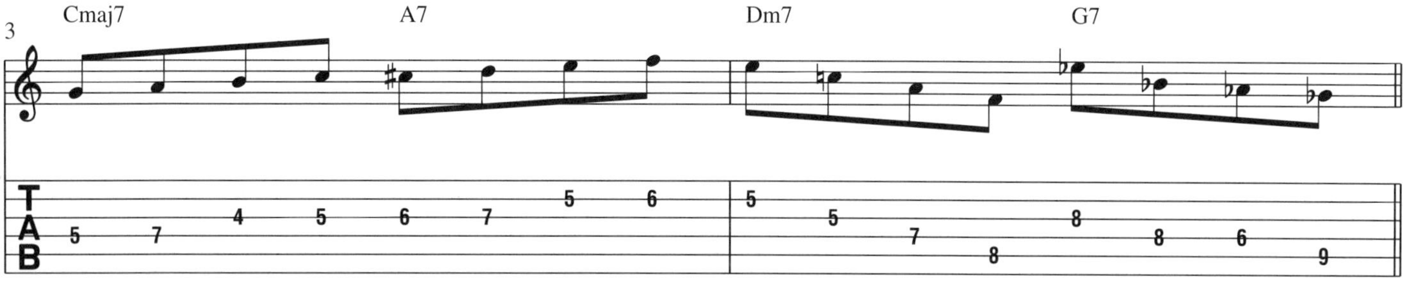

Turnarounds Starting on the 5th of the Imaj7 Chord

Turnarounds Starting on the 5th of the Imaj7 Chord

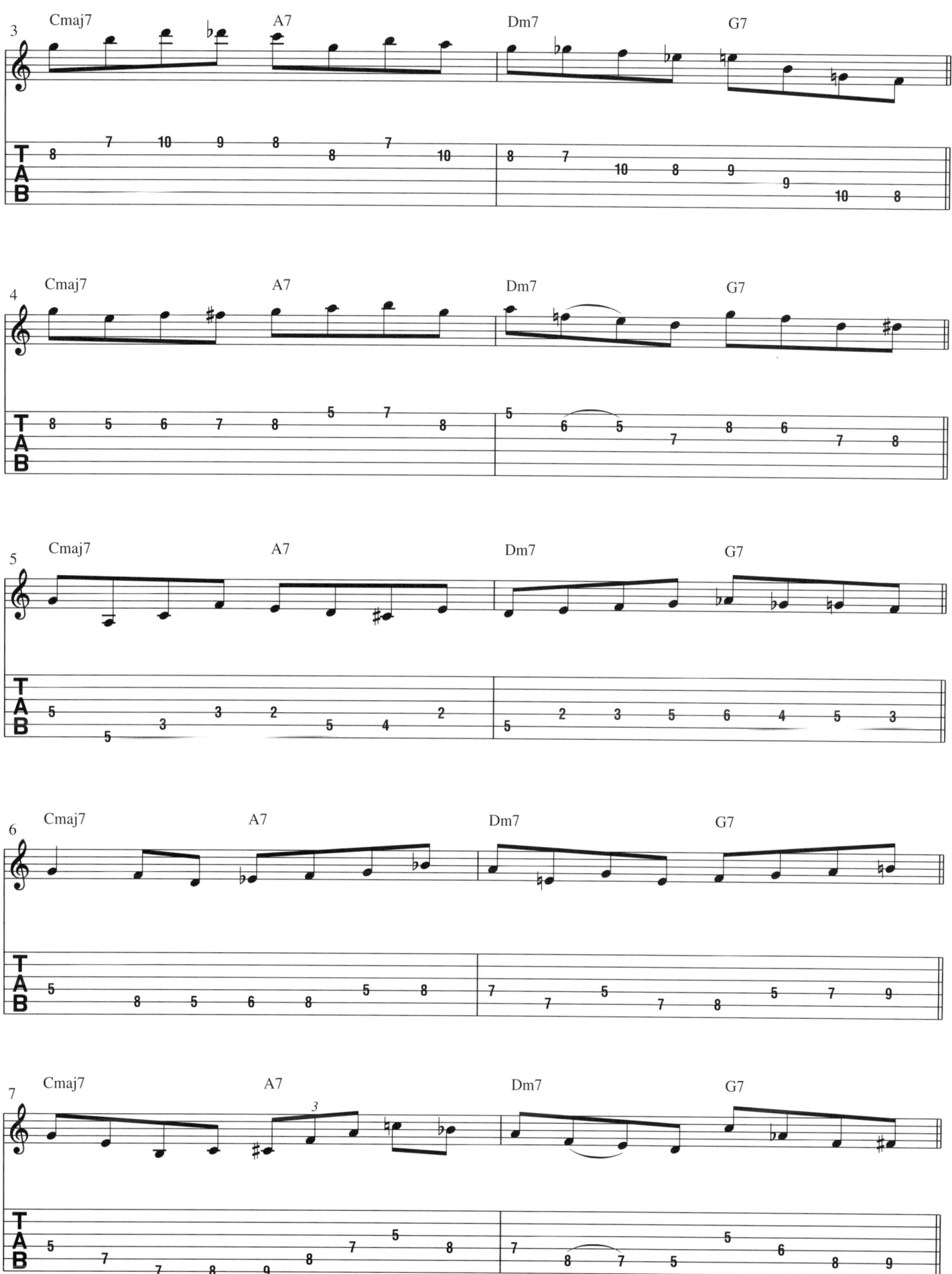

101

IDEA SUBSTITUTION CHART

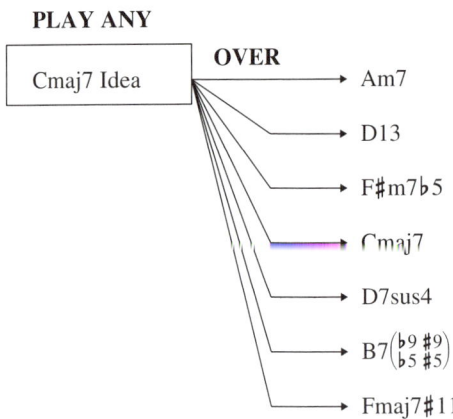

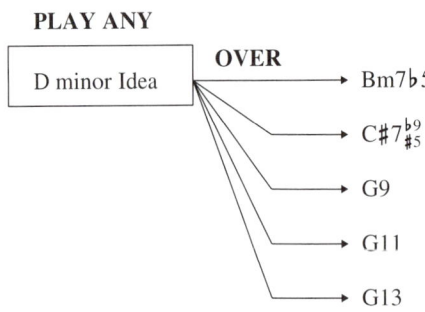

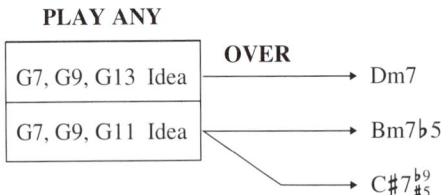

ABOUT THE AUTHOR

For over a decade, Les Wise has been gaining recognition as one of the nation's outstanding guitarists...and that recognition is well deserved.

Les was born in the Spring of 1948 in New Orleans, Louisiana. His musical training began twelve years later when he picked up the guitar. During his early years, Les studied with Joe Pass, John Gray, and Roger Filiberto, so by the time he entered the Naval School of Music in 1965, he was well prepared.

After spending most of his four years in the Navy as a member of the Naval Band, Les received an Honorable Discharge and settled in Chicago. It was here that some big name band leaders began to notice this talented, young musician. In only two years in Chicago, Les performed in the bands of Les Brown, David Rose, Woody Herman (behind singer Jack Jones), and Harry James.

Toward the end of 1970, Les was wooed away from the Chicago jazz scene to go on the road as Musical Director for variety performer John Bach. After two years of touring, Les returned to his hometown of New Orleans. It wasn't long before word of the now experienced Wise was all over town. In no time at all, Les Wise was recognized as one of the top musicians in the "birthplace of jazz." When a guitarist was needed anywhere in town, it was a pretty sure bet that the phone at the Wise household would be rining.

This notariety gave Les an opportunity to branch out into many new areas. Local producers began to use him on many recording sessions, including commercial jingle dates for Ford Motor Company, American Motors, Gulf-Western, Lever Brothers, Alka-Seltzer, The National Football League, Sunkist, E.F. Hutton, IBM, Bell Telephone, Exxon, and Standard oil. Local educators also realized that Les' experience could be useful in the classroom. As it turned out, Les proved to be particularly skillful at conveying his experience to younger players, and he was hired as a resident instructor at Loyola University in New Orleans.

Having conquered all of the musical plateaus of New orleans, Les decided in 1977 to take his family to the West Coast. Not surprisingly, his talents were again immediately noticed. In Los Angeles, he began playing with many jazz greats, including Leroy Vinnegar, Sherman Ferguson, Joe Diorio, Eugene Wright, Jack McDuff, Ernie Watts, Jimmy Smith, Max Roach, Willie Bobo, Ronnie Foster, Harold Land, Dwight Dickerson, Bob Maze, Joe Sample, Bob Magnusson, Roy McCurdy, Ted Hawk, and Howard Roberts. It was Howard Roberts who also discovered Les' talents as an educator and hired him as a staff instructor at the Guitar Institute of Technology (G.I.T.).

In a town already bursting at the seams with talented guitarists, Les had no trouble breaking into the studios. His guitar work was heard on radio and television for Levi's Jeans, Coca-Cola, Seven-Up, Max Factor, Von's Market, Alpha Beta Markets, and Ralph's. The West Coast music community really took notice when Les was named the outstanding act at the 1978 Orange County Jazz Festival.

Les Wise is known and respected across the country as an outstanding musician, educator, and author of *Inner Jazz*, *Bebop Bible*, co-author of *Ten*, and columnist in *International Musician* and *Recording World*. There really is no way to describe his technical skill and musical sensitivity. To fully appreciate the kind of musician he is, you have to hear him play.

Get Better At Guitar

...with These Great Guitar Instruction Books from Hal Leonard!

DON'T FRET NOTE MAP
REVOLUTIONARY GUITAR FINGER POSITIONING GUIDE
• created by Nicholas Ravagni
It's never been easier to learn to play guitar! For beginners just starting out or experienced guitarists who want to learn to read music, the *Don't Fret Note Map*™ will give players the tools they need to locate notes on the guitar. This revolutionary finger positioning guide fits all electric and acoustic guitars with no adhesive or fasteners, shows the note names and locations all over the fretboard and uses a unique color-coded method to make note-reading easy. The accompanying booklet includes full instructions and four easy songs to let players practice their new-found skills!
00695587 ....$9.95

Also available:
DON'T FRET CHORD MAP™
REVOLUTIONARY GUITAR FINGER POSITIONING GUIDE
• created by Nicholas Ravagni
00695670 ....$9.95

GUITAR DIAL 9-1-1
50 WAYS TO IMPROVE YOUR PLAYING ... NOW!! • by Ken Parille
Need to breathe new life into your guitar playing? This book is your admission into the Guitar ER! You'll learn to: expand your harmonic vocabulary; improvise with chromatic notes; create rhythmic diversity; improve your agility through helpful drills; supply soulful fills; create melodic lines through chord changes; and much more! The accompanying CD includes 99 demonstration tracks.
00695405 Book/CD Pack..................................$16.95

GUITAR TECHNIQUES • by Michael Mueller
Guitar Techniques is a terrific reference and teaching companion, as it clearly defines and demonstrates how to properly execute cool moves ranging from bending, vibrato and legato to tapping, whammy bar and playing with your teeth! The CD contains 92 demonstration tracks in country, rock, pop and jazz styles. Essential techniques covered include: Fretting • Strumming • Trills • Picking • Vibrato • Tapping • Bends • Harmonics • Muting • Slides • and more.
00695562 Book/CD Pack..................................$14.95

THE GUITARIST'S SURVIVAL KIT
EVERYTHING YOU NEED TO KNOW TO BE A WORKING MUSICIAN
• by Dale Turner
From repertoire to accompaniment patterns to licks, this book is fully stocked to give you the confidence knowing you can "get by" and survive, regardless of the situation. The book covers: songs and set lists; gear; rhythm riffs in styles from blues to funk to rock to metal; lead licks in blues, country, jazz & rock styles; transposition and more. The CD features 99 demonstration tracks, and the book includes standard notation and tab.
00695380 Book/CD Pack..................................$14.95

LEFT-HANDED GUITAR
THE COMPLETE METHOD • by Troy Stetina
Attention all Southpaws: it's time to turn your playing around! We're proud to announce that our groundbreaking guitar method solely devoted to lefties is now available with a CD! Complete with photos, diagrams and grids designed especially for the left-handed player, this book/CD pack teaches fundamentals such as: chords, scales, riffs, strumming; rock, blues, fingerpicking and other styles; tuning and theory; reading standard notation and tablature; and much more!
00695630 Book/CD Pack..................................$14.95
00695247 Book Only.......................................$9.95

PICTURE CHORD ENCYCLOPEDIA
PHOTOS & DIAGRAMS FOR 2,600 GUITAR CHORDS!
The most comprehensive guitar chord resource ever! Beginning with helpful notes on how to use the book, how to choose the best voicings and how to construct chords, this extensive, 272-page source for all playing styles and levels features five easy-to-play voicings of 44 chord qualities for each of the twelve musical keys – 2,640 chords in all! For each, there is a clearly illustrated chord frame, as well as *an actual photo* of the chord being played! Includes info on basic fingering principles, open chords and barre chords, partial chords and broken-set forms, and more. Great for all guitarists!
00695224 ....$19.95

SCALE CHORD RELATIONSHIPS
A GUIDE TO KNOWING WHAT NOTES TO PLAY – AND WHY!
• by Michael Mueller & Jeff Schroedl
Scale Chord Relationships teaches players how to determine which scales to play with which chords, so guitarists will never have to fear chord changes again! This book/CD pack explains how to: recognize keys; analyze chord progressions; use the modes; play over nondiatonic harmony; use harmonic and melodic minor scales; use symmetrical scales such as chromatic, whole-tone and diminished scales; incorporate exotic scales such as Hungarian major and Gypsy minor; and much more!
00695563 Book/CD Pack..................................$14.95

FOR MORE INFORMATION, SEE YOUR LOCAL MUSIC DEALER, OR WRITE TO:

7777 W. BLUEMOUND RD. P.O. BOX 13819 MILWAUKEE, WI 53213

Visit Hal Leonard Online at
www.halleonard.com

PRICES, CONTENTS AND AVAILABILITY
SUBJECT TO CHANGE WITHOUT NOTICE.

7-STRING GUITAR
AN ALL-PURPOSE REFERENCE FOR NAVIGATING YOUR FRETBOARD
• by Andy Martin
Introducing *7-String Guitar*, the first-ever method book written especially for seven-stringed instruments. It teaches chords, scales and arpeggios, all as they are adapted for the 7-string guitar. It features helpful fingerboard charts, and riffs & licks in standard notation and tablature to help players expand their sonic range in any style of music. It also includes an introduction by and biography of the author, tips on how to approach the book, a guitar notation legend, and much more!
00695508 ....$12.95

TOTAL ROCK GUITAR
A COMPLETE GUIDE TO LEARNING ROCK GUITAR • by Troy Stetina
Total Rock Guitar is a unique and comprehensive source for learning rock guitar, designed to develop both lead and rhythm playing. This book/CD pack covers: getting a tone that rocks; open chords, power chords and barre chords; riffs, scales and licks; string bending, strumming, palm muting, harmonics and alternate picking; all rock styles; and much more. The examples in the book are in standard notation with chord grids and tablature, and the CD includes full-band backing for all 22 songs.
00695246 Book/CD Pack..................................$17.95

THE GUITAR F/X COOKBOOK
• by Chris Amelar
The ultimate source for guitar tricks, effects, and other unorthodox techniques. This book demonstrates and explains 45 incredible guitar sounds using common stomp boxes and a few unique techniques, including: pick scraping, police siren, ghost slide, church bell, jaw harp, delay swells, looping, monkey's scream, cat's meow, race car, pickup tapping, and much more.
00695080 Book/CD Pack..................................$14.95

BLUES YOU CAN USE
• by John Ganapes
A comprehensive source designed to help guitarists develop both lead and rhythm playing. Covers: Texas, Delta, R&B, early rock and roll, gospel, blues/rock and more. Includes 21 complete solos; chord progressions and riffs; turnarounds; moveable scales and more. CD features leads and full band backing.
00695007 Book/CD Pack..................................$19.95

JAZZ RHYTHM GUITAR
THE COMPLETE GUIDE • by Jack Grassel
This book/CD pack by award-winning guitarist and distinguished teacher Jack Grassel will help rhythm guitarists better understand: chord symbols and voicings; comping styles and patterns; equipment, accessories and set-up; the fingerboard; chord theory; and much more. The accompanying CD includes 74 full-band tracks.
00695654 Book/CD Pack..................................$19.95